BERLIN BLOCKADE

SOVIET CHOKEHOLD AND THE GREAT ALLIED AIRLIFT 1948–1949

GERRY VAN TONDER

Pen & Sword
MILITARY

For Colonel Dudley Wall MSM, MMM, friend and brother-in-arms

First published in Great Britain in 2017 by
PEN AND SWORD MILITARY
an imprint of
Pen and Sword Books Ltd
47 Church Street
Barnsley
South Yorkshire S70 2AS

Copyright © Gerry van Tonder, 2017

ISBN 978 1 52670 826 7

Typeset by Aura Technology and Software Services, India
Maps, drawings and militaria in the colour section by Colonel Dudley Wall
Printed and bound in Malta by Gutenberg

Pen & Sword Books Ltd incorporates the imprints of Pen & Sword
Archaeology, Atlas, Aviation, Battleground, Discovery, Family History, History, Maritime, Military,
Naval, Politics, Railways, Select, Social History, Transport, True Crime, Claymore Press, Frontline Books,
Leo Cooper, Praetorian Press, Remember When, Seaforth Publishing and Wharncliffe.

For a complete list of Pen and Sword titles please contact
Pen and Sword Books Limited
47 Church Street, Barnsley, South Yorkshire, S70 2AS, England
email: enquiries@pen-and-sword.co.uk
website: www.pen-and-sword.co.uk

CONTENTS

Timeline 1945–1949   5

Dramatis Personae   8

Introduction   12

1. 'I Can Hear the Red Army Tank Calls'   16

2. A Cigarette Economy   25

3. High-Stakes Gamesmanship   39

4. Flight of the Gooney Bird   54

5. Cold Winter, Cold Relations   86

6. Small Movements of the Boa Constrictor   99

7. At What Cost?   120

Acknowledgements   127

About the Author   128

Below, far below, lies the earth that I love;
And this, my machine, is an alien thing
In these beautiful, desolate places above;
Outclimbing, outstripping the birds on the wing.

—Flight Sergeant L. N. Fox, RAF, Missing in Action, 1943

Berlin Airlift Memorial, National Memorial Arboretum, Alrewas, England.
(Courtesy Philip Nixon ARPS)

TIMELINE 1945–1949

1945

4–11 February: Heads of government – Churchill, Roosevelt and Stalin – meet at Yalta on the Black Sea to discuss the complexion of a post-war Europe.

12 April: US President Roosevelt dies and is succeeded by Truman.

21 April–2 May: Red Army under Zhukov takes Berlin.

1–4 July: Allied troops withdraw westward to their predesignated occupation zones.

17 July–2 August: Soviet, British and American heads of government and foreign ministers meet at Potsdam, Germany, to discuss the effects and consequences of the war.

6 August: American atom bomb vaporizes the Japanese city of Hiroshima.

9 August: America drops a second atom bomb over Nagasaki.

11 September–2 October: The Council of Foreign Ministers hold their first meeting in London.

30 November: A formal agreement is signed regulating the Allied air corridors in and out of Berlin.

1946

20 January: The first democratic elections are held in Germany since 1933, when Hitler had assumed dictatorial leadership of Nazi Germany.

1 September: The first local government elections are held in the Russian zone.

15 September: The British and French hold the first local government elections in their occupation zones.

1947

1 January: The American and British zones form an economic union: Bizonia.

12 March: Truman's anti-communist doctrine is announced.

5 June: American Secretary of State, George Marshall, makes public a strategy for the economic rehabilitation of Europe: the Marshall Plan.

1948

1 January: The Soviets impose stricter controls on the flow of traffic in and out of Berlin and the occupation zones.

14 January: The Soviet authorities cancel all licensed travel between the Soviet zone and those of the Allies.

24–26 January: Red Army border guards stop, search and generally harass British military trains travelling to Berlin.

1 March: A central German bank is established in the Western zones.

17 March: The Treaty of Brussels is drawn up to facilitate a defence pact between Britain, France and the Benelux countries.

20 March: The Soviet representatives walk out of the Allied Control Council. The first embargo on road and water transport routes into Allied Berlin is imposed by the Russians.

5 April: A British passenger airliner and a Soviet fighter collide above RAF Gatow. There are no survivors.

20 April: The Russians introduce barge-travel restrictions.

24 April: The Soviet authorities stop civilian passenger traffic from the Western zones into Berlin.

25 April: The Soviets introduce strict new freight documentation for goods crossing the Soviet zone into western Berlin.

1 June: Train traffic is halted between the Western zones and Berlin.

12 June: All Allied rail traffic destined for Berlin is halted.

18 June: Passenger train and mail services into Berlin are suspended.

23–24 June: The Soviet-controlled defensive Warsaw Pact is formed.

24 June: The start of the Berlin blockade: the Russians close all land and sea routes from the Allied zones to Berlin. Electricity and coal supplies to western Berlin from the east are cut off.

25 June: The first American aircraft unofficially carries food into Berlin.

26 June: The American airlift, codenamed Operation *Vittles*, commences.

28 June: The British introduce their own airlift shuttle into Berlin, calling the project Operation *Knicker*.

30 June: The Russians abandon the Four-Power government.

6 July: A diplomatic 'note' from the Allies calls for an immediate lifting of the Soviet embargo.

12 July: Construction work commences on a second runway at Tempelhof.

16 July: Work on the concrete runway at Gatow is completed.

27 July: Lancastrian tankers become the first civilian aircraft to operate in the airlift.

2 August: Western ambassadors meet with Stalin in Moscow to discuss the Berlin impasse.

5 August: Construction of a new airport at Tegel commences.

30 August: Stalin states that he will reconsider the blockade if the Western authorities withdraw their currency.

31 August: The Four-Power military governors meet for the first time since March 1947.

7 September: Irreconcilable differences cause the break-up of the Four-Power meeting.

26 September: South African Air Force aircrews arrive, the first from the British Commonwealth.

4 October: The Allies table the Berlin question before the UN Security Council.

20 October: Berlin's street lights are switched off to conserve already low electricity supplies.

26 October: The Soviet Union exercises its right to veto against a UN resolution calling on them to lift the blockade.

5 December: Construction of a second runway at Tegel commences.

15 December: Flying-boat operations into Berlin stopped.

1949

18 January: The Allies tighten their own counter-blockade.

20 March: The Western authorities declare the deutschmark the only legal tender.

4–8 April: The North Atlantic Treaty Organization – NATO – is formed in Washington.

16–17 April: Relief freight flown in a twenty-four-hour period reaches a record 13,000 tons, bringing the total to date to over 1,000,000 tons.

4 May: In New York a fresh Four-Power agreement is signed calling for the removal of all restrictions on the movement of goods and passengers from the Western zones to the Allies' sectors in Berlin.

12 May: The Soviet Military Administration in Germany, SMAD, orders the lifting of the Berlin blockade.

16 August: British civilian aircraft are withdrawn from the airlift.

30 September: The official end of the airlift.

7 October: The last RAF airlift sortie is made by a Hastings.

DRAMATIS PERSONAE

Clement Richard Attlee

'Russian Communism is the illegitimate child of Karl Marx and Catherine the Great.'

Attlee (1883–1967), British Prime Minister from 1945–1951, succeeded Winston Churchill in a landslide Labour Party victory in 1945. During his term of office, India, Pakistan, Burma and Ceylon became independent, and the mandates over Palestine and Jordan terminated. An ardent protagonist of the American-funded Marshall Plan to reconstruct Western Europe, Attlee vigorously opposed Russian communism's expansion to the west. To this end, he strongly supported a European pact to counter this threat, and would later commission Britain's nuclear deterrent.

Winston Leonard Spencer Churchill

'From Stettin in the Baltic to Trieste in the Adriatic, an iron curtain has descended across the continent.'

The British wartime Prime Minister, Churchill (1874–1965), was staunchly anti-communist and would repeatedly voice his concerns in public over the threat of Russian hegemony in Europe, dubbing it the 'Iron Curtain'. Conservative Churchill was liberal with his public praise of Labour MP Ernest Bevin and his colleagues for the successful airlift, adding that Russia was more formidable than Nazi Germany.

BOMB BERLIN

Sir – It is heartening to read of our raids on Lübeck, Rostock, the Skoda Works, and so on. Let them continue and multiply.

While not relaxing for a moment our policy of bombing industrial objectives, could we not now spare a few bombs for the important political centres, and thereby attack the enemy's morale? Such places as Berlin, Munich, Leipzig, and Nuremberg come to the mind.

Berlin has had so far about 50 raids compared with London's 500. Could anyone argue that the Reichstag at 3pm last Sunday was not a 'military objective'?

W. N. Parry, Charlton Kings, *Gloucestershire Echo*,
Tuesday 28 April 1942

(The Reichstag reference was the last meeting of Hitler's parliament, which had assembled in the Kroll Opera House on 26 April. Presided over for the full duration of the Third Reich by Reichsmarschall Hermann Göring, the session unanimously promulgated an edict making Hitler 'Supreme Judge of the German People'.)

Ernest Bevin

'...no alternative between that and surrender, and none of us can accept surrender.' (speaking of the airlift)

A trade union leader, Labour politician, and Secretary of State for Foreign Affairs from 1945 to 1951, Bevin (1881–1951) had held the office of general secretary of the influential Transport and General Workers' Union from 1922 to 1940. As wartime Minister of Labour, and unswervingly anti-communist, Bevan had a particular loathing of Russian Foreign Minister Vyacheslav Molotov, with whom he often clashed during the Berlin crisis. Bevin played a key role in the formulation of both the Marshall Plan and the North Atlantic Treaty Organisation (NATO). He worked closely with Prime Minister Attlee to produce Britain's atomic bomb.

Field Marshal Bernard Law Montgomery

'Nice chap, no General.' (speaking of Eisenhower)

A veteran of the First World War and hero of the Western Desert campaign where he defeated the German forces in North Africa during the Second World War, Montgomery (1887–1976) continued to play a major role in the liberation of Europe. Commander of Allied ground forces during the D-Day landings in June 1944, Montgomery remained at the helm of the 21st Army Group as it pushed eastwards to Germany. Upon the cessation of hostilities, he was appointed commander-in-chief of the British Army of the Rhine, the official title of the British occupation forces. Subsequently, Montgomery became chief of the Imperial general staff, and acted as General Eisenhower's deputy in the formation process of NATO.

General Sir Brian Hubert Robertson

'Rations were short in England, too, and it was no easy thing to persuade the government to spend large sums of money on feeding Germans.'

Robertson (1896–1974), a First World War recipient of the Military Cross, retired from active service in 1934, but re-enlisted in South Africa with the outbreak of the Second World War. By 1947, he had become a full general, and took up an appointment as military governor, commander-in-chief, and British member of the Allied Control Council for Germany. Robertson was Britain's first high commissioner in Germany, serving from 1949 to 1950.

Harry S. Truman

'We have to get tough with the Russians. They don't know how to behave. They are like bulls in a china shop.'

Truman (1884–1972) became American president upon the death of Franklin D. Roosevelt in April 1945. History will remember Truman as the man who first resorted to the use of nuclear weapons in conflict. He pursued a robust foreign policy based on international engagement, giving rise to his Truman Doctrine on the containment of communism, as well as the $13 billion Marshall Plan fund for the rebuilding of post-war Europe. A founder member of the United Nations, Truman oversaw the Berlin Airlift and the formation of NATO in 1949.

Franklin Delano Roosevelt

'The Soviet Union, as everybody who has the courage to face the fact knows, is run by a dictatorship as absolute as any other dictatorship in the world.'

Roosevelt (1882–1945) served as president of the United States from 1933 until his death in 1945. Overcoming polio, he cemented his place in American history with his New Deal package to tackle the economic depression of the early 1930s. Prior to the Japanese attack on Pearl Harbour in December 1941, which would plunge America into the global conflagration, Roosevelt saw his neutral nation as the 'arsenal of democracy', supplying war materiel to the Allies. Roosevelt's participation in roundtable discussions and decisions made with his British, Russian and Chinese counterparts would forever change the world's balance of power.

General Dwight David 'Ike' Eisenhower

'Steady Monty. You can't speak to me like that. I'm your boss.' (addressing Montgomery)

President of the United States from 1953, Eisenhower (1890–1969) was, with the rank of five-star general, Supreme Commander of Allied Forces in Europe during the Second World War. He was responsible for both the invasions of North Africa in 1942–43 and Europe in 1944. He became NATO's first supreme commander. The antithesis of his British counterpart, Field Marshal Montgomery, the two supremos seldom saw eye to eye pertaining to the manner in which Europe had to be liberated.

General Lucius Dubignon 'The Kaiser' Clay

'I believe the future of democracy requires us to stay here until forced out.' (speaking of Berlin)

At the end of the war in 1945, Clay (1898–1978) was serving as Eisenhower's deputy. In 1947, he assumed the position of military governor of occupied Germany. Whilst Clay became known for his administration of Germany, in which he promoted democratic federalism, he controversially commuted death sentences on some convicted Nazi war criminals. Two days after Russia introduced the Berlin blockade, Clay ordered the commencement of the airlift.

COCKTAILS BEAT TANKS

British and Australians have been tackling German tanks round Tobruk with Molotov Cocktails exactly like those made by the Home Guard in Britain.

The defenders of Tobruk have been discovering that the tank can be mastered by the individual soldier. Their tactics have been to take a steel or iron bar, jump on the tank, smash the caterpillar tractor and then throw a 'Molotov Cocktail' through the ventilators.

The 'cocktails', which are bottles filled with petrol and carrying a fuse, are being made by the Tobruk garrison.

British United Press, 16 May 1941

(It would be thirteen months before combined German and Italian forces under *Generalleutnant* Erwin Rommel eventually captured Tobruk, capturing 35,000 Allied troops.)

Joseph Vissarionovich 'Uncle Joe' Stalin

'So the bastard's dead. Too bad we didn't capture him alive.' (speaking of Hitler)

Born Losif Vissarionovich Dzhugashvili, Stalin (1878–1953) assumed the moniker Stalin – man of steel – during his formative revolutionary days in the early 1900s. Effectively a dictator, Stalin led the Soviet Union from 1922 until his death in 1953. He would ensure that Russia emerged from the war as a second super power, the nation's growing nuclear capabilities solidifying this status. Stalin's uncompromising management of the Berlin crisis spawned what became known as the Cold War.

Vyacheslav Mikhailovich Molotov

'What happens to Berlin, happens to Germany; what happens to Germany, happens to Europe.'

Molotov (1890–1986), Stalin's protégé, was the Soviet minister of foreign affairs from 1939 to 1949, and then again from 1953 to 1956. Recognised for his diplomatic skills, Molotov was instrumental in the signing of a short-lived non-aggression pact with Nazi Germany in 1939, an agreement which paved the way for Hitler's invasion of Poland. An antagonist of the Marshall Plan, which he contended had polarised Europe into two political ideologies – Imperial and Communist – Molotov initiated the Molotov Plan, which would secure Russia's relationship with Eastern European nations.

Georgi Konstantinovich Zhukov

'The mere existence of atomic weapons implies the possibility of their use.'

Zhukov (1896–1974) was a career soldier from the time he was conscripted in 1915. Marshal of the Soviet Union, he was proclaimed a Hero of the Soviet Union, and was one of only two Russians to have been awarded the Gold Star Medal four times – the other was Leonid Brezhnev. In November 1944, Zhukov was appointed commander of the 1st Belorussian Front, which took part in the taking of Berlin, exhorting his troops to 'exact a brutal revenge [on the Germans] for everything'. He was the Soviet's first commander of the Soviet Occupation Zone in Germany, where he established close working relationships with the Allied commanders, especially Eisenhower. Stalin, however, believing Zhukov had designs on his position, replaced him with Sokolovsky in 1946 and shipped the popular general off to Odessa.

Vasily Danilovich Sokolovsky

'You should be informed that the Soviet Union officially regards Hitler as dead.'

First enlisted in the Red Army in 1918, Sokolovsky (1897–1968) had been chief of staff of the Western Front in the winter of 1941 when he coordinated the successful stalling of the German advance on Moscow. Later, as chief of staff of the 1st Ukrainian Front, Sokolovsky played a role in the planning and execution of the taking of Berlin. In 1946, he was made a Marshal of the Soviet Union and appointed to the head of the Soviet Military Administration in occupied Germany.

INTRODUCTION

'Sir, I am unable to accept the view that the Berlin airlift is a "magnificent expedient". Our position resembles that of a house owner prevented from entering through his front door by a bully, and content to climb in and out by the window. The bully cannot put the matter right by offering to allow the use of the door after the house is handed over to him.'

P. H. Campbell, Exmouth, the *Western Morning News*, Tuesday 28 September 1948

In his seminal autobiography, *Mein Kampf*, Adolf Hitler leaves the reader in no doubt whatsoever that his two greatest hates in life, and therefore to be seen as obstructive threats to his vision of a Third Reich New Order, were Communism and Semitism. Equally, Hitler viewed the parliamentary system with abject disdain. He would ruthlessly dismantle the Weimar parliament, a viper pit of Jews, Social Democrats and Marxists.

The mantra of the future Fuhrer's foreign policy dovetailed perfectly with his desire to wipe Jews and communists from the face of the planet. For the Nazi dictator, adequate *lebensraum* – 'living room' – was the inalienable birthright of the German race, and Hitler insisted that 'Germany must find the courage to gather our people, and their strength, for an advance along the road that will lead this people from its present, restricted living-space to new land and soil'.

And there could only be one way to satisfy the imperative that was *lebensraum*: 'We take up where we broke off six hundred years ago. We stop the endless German movement to the south

---

RUSSIA MAY BE HITLER'S BIGGEST PROBLEM

Mysterious Russia may yet present Hitler with his biggest problem. In the isolation of the Kremlin, Joseph Stalin is said to be 'thinking things over', wondering if the time has not come for a gesture to the Allies.

If it is true that Sir William Seeds may return shortly to his ambassadorial post in Moscow, events must be taking a new turn. Diplomatic activity has been resumed in London between the Soviet and the British governments, and it is not our policy to drive the Soviet into still closer alliance with Germany, despite our natural abhorrence of Russia's ruthlessness.

There is no time for *amour propre*. At the same time, it is necessary to leave the Soviet under no illusion about the danger, indeed, the inevitably, of her being involved in European war if she moves her troops to Bessarabia [historic region in Moldova and the Ukraine] or commits any other acts of aggression. The impression given in the diplomatic reports to many Chancelleries is that Stalin is not disposed to embark on further hazardous enterprises after the shock the Finns gave him and his armies. Soviet aloofness from Germany gives definite encouragement to that belief.

Western Mail, Saturday, 30 March 1940

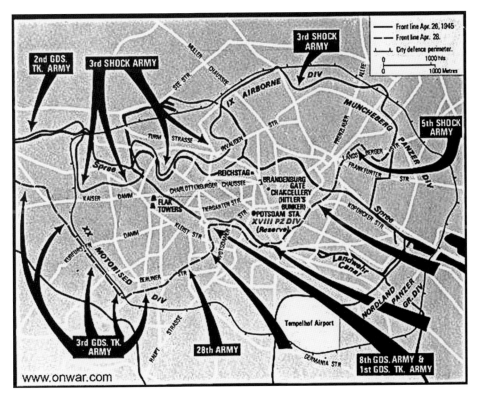

A contemporary map showing the Red Army enveloping Berlin by the end of April 1945.

and west, and turn our gaze toward the land in the East. At long last, we break off the colonial and commercial policy of the pre-war period and shift to the soil policy of the future. If we speak of soil in Europe today, we can primarily have in mind only Russia and her vassal border states.'

Europe, however, was not ready for Hitler. In September 1938, British premier Neville Chamberlain returned home from a meeting with Hitler in Munich, clutching a sheet of paper signed by Herr Hitler guaranteeing 'peace for our time'. Six months later, Hitler reneged on the agreement.

Meanwhile, Russian head of state, Joseph Stalin, was negotiating for a treaty with Britain and France. The wily Georgian-born communist, his designs on the Baltic states of Latvia, Estonia and Lithuania, needed Hitler to look the other way while he claimed these territories.

On 23 August 1939, in a move that would be construed farcical had it not been for the tragic outcome, Hitler's foreign minister, Joachim von Ribbentrop, visited Moscow to sign a German–Soviet non-aggression pact with his Soviet equivalent, Vyacheslav Molotov. A week later, Hitler's armies steamrolled their way into Poland.

Hitler's unfettered loathing of the Bolsheviks to the east, however, could only be sated with the completion of his Blitzkrieg subjugation of Western Europe. At a meeting with his military chiefs on 31 July 1940, Hitler aired his single-minded desire: 'Wiping out the very power to exist of Russia. That is the goal!'

In the autumn of 1941, Hitler launched Operation *Barbarossa*, thrusting 3,400,000 troops, 1,945 aircraft and 3,000 tanks into the Soviet Union, along a massive front extending from the Baltic Sea in the north to the Black Sea in the south.

The mutual hatred between aggressor and defender manifested itself on both sides in the form of a total disregard for the cost in human lives – numbers soared into millions within weeks. Russia's civilian population suffered death and degradation at the hands of German troops loyally following their Fuhrer's instruction to regard the Soviet population as subhuman and unfit to live. By the end of 1941, Hitler's death squads – *Einsatzgruppen* – had conducted more than sixty pogroms of genocide against Soviet Jews.

Understandably, the exact number of Soviets who lost their lives from 1941 to 1945 is still a subject of debate, but it is reckoned that Stalin's 'Great Patriotic War' to defend Russia claimed the lives of 15 million civilians and 10 million soldiers.

Retribution would be Stalin's.

The price of Hitler's transgressions in Russia would be extracted from the German people. Hate propaganda and a burning desire – frequently alcohol-induced – to avenge German atrocities in Russia resulted in the conquering Red Army conducting widespread mass rapes of German girls and women – estimates range up to 2 million.

Some historians argue that Stalin did not order, let alone condone, the violent behaviour of his troops in Germany. The Soviet dictator, however, certainly did not appear to discourage the Red Army's excesses – his attentions were fixed on claiming the spoils of war as agreed to at various Allied conferences. He would indelibly imprint Socialism on his territorial prizes, including his share of Hitler's citadel. He was the liberator who rid the world of Nazi fascism, the winner of the race to Berlin.

The signing of the German instrument of surrender in Reims on 7 May 1945, therefore, irked Stalin. His forces had captured Germany as far west as the River Elbe, including the whole of the city of Berlin. In his memoirs, Marshal Zhukov quotes Stalin:

> Today, in Reims, Germans signed the preliminary act on an unconditional surrender. The main contribution, however, was done by Soviet people and not by the Allies, therefore the capitulation must be signed in front of the Supreme Command of all countries of the anti-Hitler coalition, and not only in front of the Supreme Command of Allied Forces. Moreover, I disagree that the surrender was not signed in Berlin, which was the centre of Nazi aggression. We agree with the Allies to consider the Reims protocol as preliminary.

The following day, in Berlin, *Generalfeldmarschall* Wilhelm Keitel signed and handed to Marshal Zhukov the terms for the surrender of the German military. Moscow was in a different time zone and the day was 9 May, a day that became, and still is, a national victory day celebration in Russia.

In those first uneasy days in May, an East–West rift had already developed between the erstwhile victors. Accusations of reneging on the Potsdam Agreement were levelled at each other by both political and ideological camps. Interpretations of the fundamental clauses of the tripartite agreement became imbedded in the divided Four-Power government and economy of Berlin.

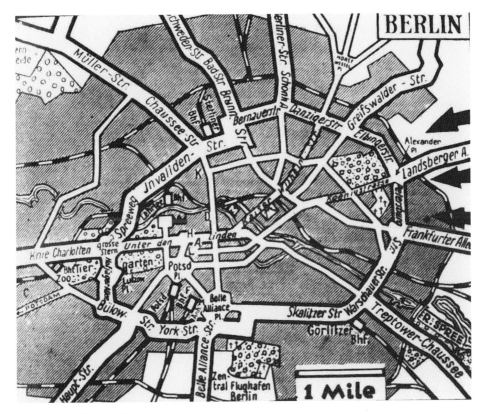

A German media map of Berlin in the late 1930s.

Positions hardened and any thoughts of compromise dissipated. Moscow was adamant that the Soviet Union legitimately won ownership of Berlin, and would therefore not accept a currency and local authority put in place by the Western allies.

What ensued was an increasingly volatile contest of diplomatic gamesmanship, military posturing and outright provocation by the Russians. Stalin badly wanted the Allies out of *his* city, to such an extent, that his actions brought Europe and the world precariously close to a catastrophic conflagration.

1. 'I CAN HEAR THE RED ARMY TANK CALLS'

Reporting for the British *Daily Mirror*, journalist David Walker had been accompanying the American Ninth Army, commanded by Lieutenant General William Simpson, as they pushed across the Elbe on 12 April 1945. Almost two weeks later, Simpson encountered the rebuilt German Twelfth *Armee* under General Walther Wenck, whose attempt to relieve the besieged Hitler, holed up in his Berlin *Führerbunker*, would be the last by the now decimated *Heer*.

On 22 April, Walker wrote, 'Beside me a 26-year-old Russian colonel is shouting the recognition signal into the field radio set. We can clearly hear the Russian tank commanders. "My tank is burning. My tank is burning," was one of the first messages picked up.'

The demise of the Third Reich was imminent and, within days, the Soviet hammer and sickle would be hoisted atop the Reichstag, symbolically asserting Russian title over Berlin.

The repercussions of this hard-fought-for communist foothold in the West would ripple down the ensuing decades, bringing with it the very real danger of a global nuclear catastrophe.

A Soviet T-34 tank crosses the River Bug in Poland.

Rueing the outcome of the race for Berlin, and thrown blindly into a cauldron of precarious diplomatic gamesmanship, the Allies looked to each other for a scapegoat to whom blame for this strategic blunder could be apportioned.

The order of battle for the 6 June 1944 Normandy landings comprised the Supreme Headquarters Allied Expeditionary Force (SHAEF), the headquarters of the commander of Allied forces in north-west Europe, General Dwight Eisenhower, with one British and two American army groups under his command. General Bernard Montgomery, after initially controlling all invading ground troops pending sufficient American troops landing, retained command of the 21st Army Group, which comprised the British Second and Canadian First armies.

More than a month after securing the eastern Gold, Juno and Sword beachheads, Montgomery, despite earlier boasts, had not been able to break out and take Caen. *Generalleutnant* Edgar Feuchtinger's 21st Panzer Division, joined within days by the murderous *Hitlerjugend* – Hitler Youth – of the 12th SS Panzer Division, doggedly resisted any attempts by Montgomery to progress any significant distance beyond the beaches. The British media, however, reported that Montgomery was waiting for the American forces to turn around and align themselves on his right flank after having overrun the Cotentin Peninsula. Completely misrepresenting the true situation – most likely out of ignorance – the *Western Mail* and *South Wales News* stated on 3 July that 'Montgomery may be content to pull his punches and allow the enemy to weaken themselves in counter-attacks which have all failed'.

The massive combined air and ground assault, Operation *Goodwood*, eventually resulted in the taking of Caen on 20 July, but dearly so in terms of loss of armour and troops. The cost of the six-week delay, and while Eisenhower and Montgomery continued to bicker, would be felt for decades to come.

3,500 PLANES IN BOMBING BLASTING

Bomber Command included in its targets for last night Gelsenkirchen, important centre of the German synthetic oil plants, which yesterday had its heaviest attack of the war. Coblenz and other Western German objectives were also hit.

Huge fires were still burning in Gelsenkirchen last night some hours after the heavy afternoon attack. Squadrons of Mosquitos bombed the town again after dark and crews reported that the fires covered a large area.

Lancasters made a saturation raid on Coblenz. The attack was all over in 10 minutes, yet in that short time great fires were started and dense smoke rose nearly 10,000 feet.

In all, something like 3,500 planes were thrown into the Allies' round-the-clock offensive yesterday. Last night's attack was the third of the day.

Earlier, the US 8th Air Force sent out more than 1,100 bombers and 700 fighters, and well over 1,000 bombers and more than 250 fighters delivered the RAF's hammer blows.

Lincolnshire Echo, Tuesday, 7 November 1944

British troops take a rest in the massive Hindenburg Bastion bunker on the Normandy beach.

On 15 July, the *Staffordshire Advertiser* had already reported that 'while our troops are battling courageously against a strong and relentless foe in Normandy ... the threat from the Eastern front grows even more menacing. The Red Army is irresistible. Day by day they are striding westward and the Germans are powerless to halt their progress. The Allied military commentators declare that Russia is certain to reach German soil first'.

On 23 June 1944, the Soviets launched Operation *Bagration* along a 450-mile front in Belorussia. With the liberation of Minsk as its first objective, the 3rd and 2nd Belorussian fronts, with support from the 1st farther south, the Reds amassed 1.7 million troops and 2,700 tanks to sweep westwards towards German-occupied Poland. Commanding the 3rd, Colonel General Ivan Chernyakhovsky carried out the much-vaunted liberation of Vilna to the north, while Marshal Konstantin K. Rokossovsky, with his 1st, executed a pincer movement from the south towards Minsk, before striking west towards Warsaw. General Ivan Petrov's Second mopped up the centre. Hitler's *Ostheer* – Eastern Army – lost 25 divisions, amounting to 350,000 troops.

At the beginning of August, Rokossovsky reached the outskirts of the Polish capital, but here he came to a halt as the Polish Home Army had come out in armed insurrection. This gallant show of Polish nationalism by the citizens of Warsaw was not well received by Stalin, so he stood back and watched as the German garrison brutally and relentlessly dealt with the uprising. Polish casualties were extreme: 15,000 of the Home Army and 225,000 civilians paid for this disobedience with their lives.

A British 5.5-inch gun trundles east, passing German military graves.

At the same time, the Allies were still in Normandy, but the media naïvely celebrated an advance of 60 miles in nine days. A 6 August German counter-attack at Mortain, a few miles south-west of Caen, proved the enemy were not yet prepared to relinquish occupied Normandy.

By mid-September, Montgomery's Second Army, together with airborne American infantry, fought what the media described as 'a slow, unspectacular slogging match along the whole of the Allied salient into Holland'. General Miles Dempsey simultaneously poured men and armour along the Eindhoven–Nijmegen road, thereby strengthening the British spearhead aimed at Arnhem.

On 17 September, Montgomery launched his ill-fated and much-criticised Operation *Market Garden*, with the strategic objective of executing an enveloping pincer movement around the Ruhr, the centre of Hitler's industry. To achieve this ambitious goal, the Allies needed to secure key bridges over the Nederrijn (Lower Rhine) and the Maas. Operation *Market Garden*, however, was an unmitigated disaster, and yet again, the Allies' advance towards Berlin was halted. *Generalfeldmarschalls* Walter Model and Gerd von Rundstedt, successive commanders of the *Oberbefehlshaber West* (German Armed Forces on the Western Front), prevented the Allies from crossing: 41,600 airborne troops, two infantry divisions, an armoured division and an armoured brigade. There were between 15,000 and 17,000 casualties, with a loss of 88 tanks and 144 transport aircraft.

Not even three months later, in a costly and ill-conceived offensive on their Western Front, the Allies lost a further six weeks in their easterly advance. Codenamed *Unternehmen Wacht am Rhein* (Operation *Watch on the Rhine*) by the Germans, journalists dubbed the December 1944 action the Battle of the Bulge. By Christmas, von Rundstedt's drive was halted, but it would take a further four weeks before the battle was officially declared over. The cost to both sides was massive: more than 200,000 casualties, 1,600 tanks and 1,450 aircraft.

Amidst reports of thousands of people fleeing Berlin, by the end of January, Russian Marshals Ivan Konev's 1st Ukrainian Front and Georgy Zhukov's 1st Belorussian Front had established several bridgeheads over the Oder and Vistula, effectively severing East Prussia from the German Fatherland. In southern Poland, Konev's armies captured Kraków.

By mid-February, Montgomery's British and Canadian armies were slowly rolling forward the Maas–Rhine Front. Nine German divisions had been encountered – the 345th the most recent – and beaten back with the aid of tactical RAF air support. After visiting some of his

Mid-February 1945, Montgomery's 21st Army Group moves through Reichswald Forest during Operation *Veritable*. A British Bren gunner watches as an AVRE Churchill tank with 290mm Petard mortar comes down the track.

troops in an open Jeep, the more relaxed Montgomery confidently claimed, 'We now come to the last and final round.'

On the afternoon of 7 March, forward units of the 9th Armoured Division of the American First Army reached the Rhine at Remagen, where they discovered that von Rundstedt had failed to destroy the Ludendorff rail bridge across the river. After a protracted struggle to prevent the Germans from destroying the bridge, the Americans crossed. The Allies finally set foot in Nazi Germany. That very day, three Orders of the Day from Stalin, true to his stated philosophy of not even trusting himself, gave no indication whatsoever of the progress of his armies on Hitler's citadel. The Soviet mass-circulation daily newspaper, *Izvestia*, however, stated that the Red Army had crossed an unnamed river and, breaking through the defences, was 'moving on Berlin'. Zhukov had crossed the Oder, and was now only 35 miles from Berlin. Two weeks later, Montgomery was massing his troops for a 'good strong heave' to at last cross the Rhine.

On 31 March, British newspapers made reference to a 'secret target' set by Eisenhower for his army commander, General Patton. It transpired that the American leader had drafted a message to Stalin informing him that the Soviets should take Berlin, while his forces concentrated on the Erfurt–Leipzig–Dresden line. Eisenhower believed that the Germans were moving their government to this area. The British were stunned at this development, and Churchill warned of dire consequences. The distrustful Stalin saw this as nothing but a bluff by the Americans. He immediately accelerated his move on Berlin, while informing the Allies that he was in fact marching west towards Leipzig.

Right: A 21st Army Group column progresses east through north Rhineland on a Sherman Firefly tank mounted with a 17-pdr anti-tank gun.

Below: US armour and troops move on the Rhine.

'In Normandy our strategy for the land battle, and the plan to achieve it, was simple and clear-cut. The pieces were closely stitched together. It was never allowed to become unstitched; and it succeeded. After Normandy, our strategy became unstitched. There was no plan; and we moved by disconnected jerks.' Montgomery in his memoirs

Three weeks later, Soviet armour entered the forest surrounding Hangelsberg, a mere 8 miles from greater Berlin's boundary. Two other Red Army columns were simultaneously making direct for the German capital, one 10 miles to the east near Strausberg and the other in the Protzel area, and now only 16 miles from the city. German Radio reported that the rumble of guns was heard in the city centre, adding that out of four million citizens, three million were still in Berlin. On 20 April, Luxemburg Radio painted a more graphic picture: 'Berlin is seething with unrest, civil war is rife, red flags have appeared on all buildings in the workers' districts, and there have been big peace demonstrations in the Reich capital and Munich.'

By the last week of April, and with the British Second Army 'continuing to strengthen their grip on the approaches to Bremen and Hamburg' more than 160 miles to the north and east of Berlin, Moscow reported that more than 20 of Berlin's suburbs had been captured, and that a fifth to a quarter of the city was now in the grip of the Russian Army.

On 23 April, a defiant German radio commentator, Dr Otto Kriegk, accused the Allies of leaving the fate of the German nation in the hands of the Russians. The report appeared in the last edition extra of the *Manchester Evening News* of that date:

British infantry check captured war materiel at a German strongpoint, Cleves, north Rhineland.

From an appeal by Dr Joseph Goebbels [Hitler's Minister of Propaganda] just made public, we know that the Führer has decided to stay in Berlin. The Führer has decided to stay in the Reich capital at this grave hour. We now tell the German people, and we tell the whole world this, and thereby kill all the fantastic rumours with which the enemy attempts to undermine the morale of the German camp. Every Berliner knows that these rumours are false and invented by the enemy camp.

Asking ourselves why Hitler stayed in Berlin we give the following answer – we children of a happy Europe, which has left us to fight Bolshevism by ourselves, will do everything in our power not only to stem the Russian advance, but to throw back the hated Bolshevist enemy.

We will never forget that the Western Allies are racing with the Russians to have the honour of extirpating the German people and culture first.

With less than 24 hours to go before the eve of the great Soviet holiday, Zhukov and Konev penetrated the heart of Berlin, pushing for a May Day victory. The Tiergarten was reached, and to the north, Zhukov pushed to within 600 yards of the Reichstag. The Soviets found much

The horrendous sight that met the Allies at Belsen Concentration Camp.

23

evidence of suicide and desertion amongst the defeated German Army. Berliners were seen plundering food stores in the smoke- and dust-laden Unter den Linden.

At 10.30 pm on 1 May, a radio broadcast from Hamburg announced that the Fuhrer had 'fallen at his post'. Grand Admiral Karl Dönitz, later *Reichspräsident* (president) of Germany, succeeded Hitler and announced in the same broadcast that 'the military struggle continues with the aim of saving the German people from Bolshevism. We shall continue to defend ourselves against the Anglo-Americans just as long as they impede our aim'. His rhetoric, however, fell on the deaf ears of a nation that had had enough.

That night, Zhukov's 150th and 171st rifle divisions continued in their drive to neutralise the remnants of a disparate group of 5,000 SS troops, *Hitlerjugend* and *Volkssturm* (end-of-war militia), who were tenaciously defending the Reichstag. The next day, one of history's most iconic photographs was taken: two Red Army soldiers hoisting the hammer-and-sickle-emblazoned red flag of the Soviet Union over the Reichstag.

Nazi Germany had been defeated. The Russian fronts under Zhukov, Konev and Rokossovsky had sustained 305,000 casualties, but for Stalin this was the necessary price of staking his claim to the city of Berlin.

MUSSOLINI SHOT IN THE BACK

Mussolini has come to an ignominious end – summarily executed by the Italian Liberation Committee at Dango, in the Province of Como, by being shot in the back as Italian War Criminal No. 1.

Fifteen of his followers were executed along with him – all shot in the back. Their bodies were exhibited in the town square and later conveyed to Milan, where they were shown to a great crowd in the Piazza Loreto, where the Fascists recently murdered fifteen patriots.

Milan Radio states that Mussolini's body, along with those of fourteen others, was hung from a petrol pump station, and one woman fired five times into the body. 'Five shots for my five assassinated sons,' she said.

Describing the crowds flocking to see the bodies, the commentator said: 'From the entrance to the piazza it is impossible to move because the crowd is so great. It is interesting to see the hate, the fury of those around Mussolini. People spit upon the body, but that is only a continuation of the justice he should have suffered. He died too quickly.'

Liverpool Daily Post, Monday, 30 April 1945

2. A CIGARETTE ECONOMY

'THE THIRD REICH IS NO MORE,' the British tabloid headlines proclaimed on 9 May 1945.

The previous day, a heavily guarded *Generalfeldmarschall* Wilhelm Keitel, Supreme Commander of the German Armed Forces, was brought before Marshal Zhukov at his headquarters in Berlin's eastern Karlshorst suburb. Keitel, who was later hanged as a war criminal at Nuremburg on 16 October 1946, signed Germany's unconditional surrender. His co-signatories were commander of the navy, *Generaladmiral* Hans-Georg von Friedeburg, who committed suicide two weeks later, and the Luftwaffe chief of general staff, *Generaloberst* Hans-Jürgen Stumpff. Released by the British in 1947, Stumpff died in Frankfurt in 1978.

In a radio broadcast, an ebullient Stalin praised his armies 'on the victorious conclusion of the Great Patriotic War'. He ordered 30 salvos from 1,000 field guns to seal the victory. It was also, however, an unsubtle message that the might of his Red Army remained intact.

The joint occupation of Berlin by the so-called Four Powers would commence as soon as Stalin gave his assent for Soviet administrators to issue British, American and French representatives with passports.

The centre of Hitler's once magnificent capital of the Fatherland had become an apocalyptic tableau of rubble, scattered fires, and intermittent explosions and gunfire. Contemporary reports spoke of a city where its burghers had largely gravitated to the suburbs to escape the carnage of the inner city.

A week after the formal surrender of the Nazi war machine, Radio Moscow announced that the Red Army has set up bakeries and shops to alleviate the dire shortage of food in

The severely damaged Reichstag.

Berlin. The city's entire commercial, trading, retail and administrative infrastructure had been levelled. Communications with outlying districts no longer existed, the water supply was severely interrupted, and electric lights only functioned in a few areas. Beneath the mountains of bricks, plaster and concrete lay unburied bodies estimated to be in the tens of thousands. The outbreak of typhoid and other related diseases posed a meaningful threat to the new occupiers.

As the summer of 1945 warmed up, Russian-controlled districts in Berlin established centres to regulate and direct labour, under the mantra 'no work, no food'. A British spokesman with the Allied forces in occupied Berlin also warned the city that British citizens would not have their rations cut to feed Germans, adding that there will be a tendency for Germans' rations to go down. Within the British sector, the military government gave the local German authorities the tonnages of bread, sugar, meat and butter needed for all displaced persons. To this was added extra ration quotas that the local authorities were required to provide for the thousands of German POWs being repatriated. Whatever food was left after these forced commitments would be for the ordinary people of Berlin. Such a miserable ration, however, would never amount to more than 1,500 calories a day, compared with the 2,600 below which the minimum British ration never sank throughout the war.

ZHUKOV AND 'IKE' SING – IN HARMONY

It was a great day for the Allied military chiefs Eisenhower, Montgomery and Zhukov at Frankfurt-on-Main yesterday.

On 'Monty' and 'Ike' Marshal Zhukov bestowed Russia's Order of Victory, glittering stars set with ninety-nine diamonds and rubies. Each is valued at £4,000.

So great is the honour that only five Russian generals have received it. Montgomery and Eisenhower are the first two non-Russians to be to be presented with it.

At the lunch which followed at Eisenhower's HQ, Zhukov started by making speeches stressing the need for Allied unity. They ended by singing in harmony. After many toasts had been drunk, coloured entertainers sang and danced, much to the delight of stocky, round-faced Marshal Zhukov.

Their last two songs were *Old Black Joe* and *Old Folks at Home*. Zhukov and Eisenhower joined in, their heads together, harmonising to the music of guitars.

In a toast to Eisenhower, Zhukov said: 'Here is a man with the heart of a soldier and the mind of a diplomat – the man who has been able to organise the many different nationalities under his command and lead them to victory. In reply, Eisenhower paid tribute to the help of the most skilful soldiers and diplomats that two great nations could provide: 'To them I owe a measurable debt of gratitude.'

The only time Montgomery spoke was when he received the decoration from Zhukov: 'I regard it as a high honour to receive this award from such a renowned marshal of the Soviet Union as Marshal Zhukov.'

Daily Mirror, Monday, 11 June 1945

Nazi Germany 5 reichsmark note.

On 6 June, the military chiefs of the four powers signed a declaration in Berlin on the defeat of Nazi Germany. An Allied Control Council was formed, but Moscow refused to give Zhukov decision-making powers in the council. The instructions to the Russian marshal were clear: there will be no further discussions until American troops are withdrawn from the proposed Soviet-controlled sector, and the British retire to the west of the Elbe. An Allied Control Council agreement would result in the Soviet Union assuming supreme control over almost half of Germany. The Allies were quick to point out, however, that the Russians would only control 15 million of Germany's total estimated population of 70 million.

The ensuing months saw the plight of Berliners becoming more pitiful by the day. Food was desperately short, and with jobs virtually non-existent, the reichsmark was as scarce. Children would raid swill bins at occupying forces' canteens, or beg *'bitte, bitte* (please, please) Tommy' for leftovers from British troops.

In many of the cities, an adult German could expect a ration of 3lb of black bread and 4oz of meat once a week. Once a month, they would receive 8oz of butter, 2oz of cheese, and 4oz of ersatz coffee. He might get two cigarettes a day if he was lucky, and women were allowed one if they were available. British and American cigarettes quickly became the new 'currency' across occupied Germany. The 'exchange rate' on the thriving black market in the latter half of 1945 was around three reichsmarks (1s. 6d.) to a cigarette. The British soldier found that relatively few cigarettes could buy quality German watches, cameras and jewellery.

As with any normal supply-and-demand-driven economy, the situation gave rise to spiralling 'selling prices'. In the space of three months, the cost of fifteen-jewelled German watches rose from 50 to 200 cigarettes. On the black market, the 200 cigarettes would get the seller 600 reichsmarks, enough to buy a pound of butter or 2lb of coffee. The ultimate symptom of utter degradation was the prevalent bartering by German women of sexual favours for a few cigarettes or a bar of chocolate.

Left: Churchill at the entrance to Hitler's Chancellery on Wilhelmstrasse, with a Russian guide who had fought with the Red Army on 2 May 1945 when they took the building.

Below: Victory cigarettes.

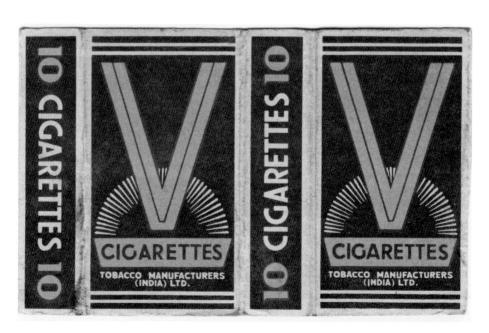

By the end of 1945, there was a massive oversupply of currency in occupied Germany: 60 billion reichsmarks and 18 billion occupation marks, the latter introduced by the Allies in 1944.

In May the following year, the British occupation authorities were forced to intervene in their sector. Financial investigations commissioned to identify the causes of spiralling inflation revealed that both military and civilian clubs, shops, canteens, theatres and other official institutions were being flooded by excess money made in black-market transactions, mainly in cigarettes. Of major concern to the Treasury was that goods purchased in sterling were being purchased with an over-abundant currency that only had a value in Germany itself.

From 1 August, all transactions in German marks in the British zone were abolished. So-called field cashiers would pay troops in sterling-denominated vouchers. British civilian and military personnel would be able to exchange their vouchers for marks, but marks could not be changed into vouchers. This was a major blow to the 'entrepreneurial' activities of many who, through black-market trading, had amassed fortunes in German and occupied marks. Many such transactions included the selling of cigarettes to nicotine-impoverished Germans for as much as 100 marks (£2 10/-) for a packet of ten.

The *Sunderland Daily Echo and Shipping Gazette* columnist Ferdinand Tuohy gave a damning indictment on 29 August 1946 under the banner, 'Europe Sick and Bleeding'. In his condemnation of the apathy of the four Allies 'with conflicting aims', he points out that in the British sector a mere 36,000 out of 162,000 homes remaining have been 'patched up'. He reserved his strongest vilification, however, for the socio-economic depravity that many of Berlin's children had been allowed to descend into by the city's vanquishers. Tuohy wrote,

The only happiness native to Berlin that I can vouch for it among its Dead End Kids, and theirs is a happiness that makes one shudder.

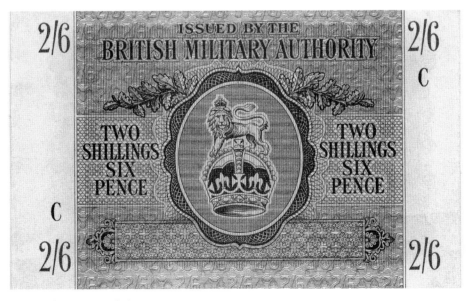

British military-occupied 2/6 note.

British military-occupied 6d note.

They have their hide-outs in the ruins, and they'll shoot if you force a way. They work in gangs, boys and girls aged mostly from 10 to 16, and their dens resemble pirates' caves. All that the troops deal in: army stores, tyres, petrol, jewellery, cigarettes, watches. How the terrible children come by them is best passed over.

Such is a quick memory of the Berlin one leaves: a wreck haunted by its flamboyant orgy of only yesterday; a place of crazy obscenity and pitiful hardship, where the old and the failing are all too often scandalously lefty to peter out: city of informers and stifled hates.

Following an extensive visit to Germany in August 1946, British MP Douglas Marshall warned of the need 'to take a firm hand with Russia unless we are to be plunged into a third world war'. In the large German cities, Marshall encountered 'the smell of death from the bunkers in which men, women and children too weak, and without the means of dabbling in the black market or supplementing their food by the ready sale of body or possessions, were living in the four square yards of space officially allotted to them'.

The Cornwall MP contended that the Soviets had not conformed to the spirit of the agreement reached by the Four Powers at Potsdam, refusing to despatch food from their zone. He referred to the bomb-devastated Berlin as a 'prostituted city', in which the British occupiers have become obsessed with a sole objective: to get the Russians to sign bits of paper that they would go on to ignore. He spoke to the *Western Morning News*:

The food position in Berlin is far better than anywhere in the British zone, but there is an open black market in which everything is based on the cigarettes. Most things can be bought for ten cigarettes.

An atmosphere such as this is not refreshing, nor is it conducive to moral behaviour. I was told that the Russians despised us; that they could not understand the value we set upon human life. They cannot understand that we object to the rape of women and children; that we disliked children being taken away from their parents for re-education in Russia.

For the Allies, the war was all but over.

> There is a wealth of difference between Great Britain and Russia, and it is far better to proceed knowing that difference is there. The iron curtain between the British and Russian zones is the same as it was when I was last in Germany six months ago and is killing a Western form of life.

That autumn, the United States started to make overtures to the Russians and French to join them and Britain in the economic unification of Germany. In a speech in Washington on 6 September 1946, Acting US Secretary of State William Clayton made reference to a possible conference by the 'Big Four' to map out a much-needed resolution to Germany's economic shambles.

In occupied Germany, however, lip service was paid to this political rhetoric thousands of miles away. The citizens of Berlin had grown their own tobacco, producing 180,000 pounds of cured tobacco at that time. This was like printing money.

Then, as local elections in Berlin approached, canvassing by the two ideologically rivalled camps unashamedly used tobacco as a prime canvassing tool. The Soviet 'manifesto' promised

Westminster cigarettes made in South Africa.

30 million cigarettes, albeit of astringent Russian blend, while the British pledged 8 million cigarettes, 492,000 cigars and 144,000 ounces of pipe tobacco. The Americans, on the other hand, appealed to the German penchant for beer by striving to win votes with an offer of 7 million pints of it.

There would be no easing in the demand for this desirable, black market organic 'currency'. In October, half a million cigarettes were stolen during four raids in four nights from the United Nations Relief and Rehabilitation Administration (UNRRA) warehouse at Camp Schleissheim near Munich. In November, a 14-year-old Berlin boy murdered an elderly woman with a kitchen knife and a truncheon to get at her cigarettes. And as another punishing year

400 STEINWAYS LIE ROTTING

Concert grand pianos, fit for the world's finest pianists, are lying rotting in the famous Steinway factory on the outskirts of Hamburg. There are only a few dozen of the famous grands completely finished, but there are 400 to 500, worth as much as £400 each, in various stages of construction. It is the most valuable store of pianos anywhere in Germany, and possibly in the world.

The four-storey Steinway factory was damaged in an air raid in October 1944, and since then it has turned out no more pianos.

'We have had virtually to stop production,' said Herr Reichart, the deputy manager. 'The floors are open to the wind and the weather.'

The value of the factory to the world of music has risen considerably during the war, since both the Blüthner factory in Leipzig and the Bechstein factory in Berlin were completely destroyed in raids.

The Press and Journal, 4 June 1945

Unter den Linden in ruins, with the Brandenburg Gate in the distance.

drew to a close for a pauperised Berlin, 'special Christmas' rations of 20 cigarettes for a man and ten for a woman were allocated.

In pursuance of an agenda drawn up at the previous meeting of the 'Big Four' foreign ministers in New York, 24 delegates, deputies and 'experts' came together in Moscow, with Soviet Foreign Minister Molotov in the chair. The prickly question about the 'denazification' of Germany and its political and economic future dominated deliberations.

While American President Truman's timing during the conference to ask Congress for American aid to Greece and Turkey was viewed by many to have been clumsily inopportune, there was a consensus in Moscow that cooperation amongst the four nations represented would be simplified by agreement on economic unity for Germany. British Foreign Minister Bevin, however, was adamant that unrestricted freedom of movement throughout all four zones was a fundamental prerequisite to 'Allied attempts at constructive peace making'.

Molotov, though, became intransigent, demanding reparations to the value of £2.5 billion and control of the industrially potent Ruhr being vested in all four powers. What came as a shock to Western delegates was Molotov's bombshell revelation that, at the Yalta Conference in February 1945, Britain, the United States and Russia had entered into a secret pact on German reparations. The Foreign Office in London confirmed that the agreement entailed stripping the defeated Germany of its local and international assets, unhindered access to production, and free use of German labour.

By the ninth day of the conference it had become clear that 'divergences between Russia and the Western powers regarding policy towards Germany' were becoming more manifest daily as the conference proceeded. Proposals for reform of the reichsmark by the foreign ministers precipitated a significant fall in the value of the German currency to 290 to the American dollar, against the official rate of ten marks.

With two years of the war still to go, German civilians flee Berlin for East Prussia.

As 1947 drew to a close, the diplomatic rift between East and West grew, characterised by open attacks and retaliations of the political doctrines of each camp. At the 7 November Great October Socialist Revolution celebrations in Red Square, Soviet minister for the armed forces, Marshal Nikolai Bulganin, declared that 'the forces of capitalism were making plans for a new imperialist war while the Soviet Union was continuing to conduct a struggle for peace and security'. It did not go unnoticed that the American military attachés to Moscow had not been invited to the Russians' massive display of might. The American ambassador had been invited, but had elected to stay away, giving the cold Soviet winter day as the

Sacks of gold. Patton's US Third Army seizes Germany's entire gold reserve near Mulhausen, April 1945.

reason. In Berlin, the American military governor, General Lucius Clay, announced that he would use the American-licensed German newspapers, such as *Der Abend*, to counter Soviet attacks on American policy and institutions.

In the first week of January 1948, the War Office declared the British armed forces special vouchers – Bafs – invalid, and instructed all British troops and civilians in the British zone to exchange their vouchers for new currency. Introduced in the summer of 1946 as an anti-inflationary measure, illegal trading in these vouchers had sent their price up to 300 marks against the official rate of forty. A new currency came into circulation on 7 January, containing wire tape and of a colour designed to defeat photocopying.

After the further failure in London of the four occupation powers to agree to a unified currency reform, Moscow ordered the Soviet military authorities to proceed with the detailed plans for separate currency reform in East Germany. In an apparent move influenced by their determination to go their own way, the Soviet authorities set the end of May or early June as the targeted implementation date. The *Tägliche Rundschau*, a newspaper published by the Red Army in the Soviet Occupation Zone, declared that the Western powers were entirely to blame for the lack of success in the negotiations for a single currency reform for the whole of occupied Germany.

Headstrong British Foreign Secretary Ernest Bevin, speaking at a Labour conference in Scarborough on 20 May, silenced his critics with his uncompromising stance towards divisive activities in Europe. The *Nottingham Evening Post* quoted from his speech:

> I cannot change the Communism of Russia, and I am not going to try. We intend, whatever provocation there might be, to stay in Berlin. We shall have a lot of provocation to put up with. I suggest for a start they might set an example and stop it. We would have been guilty of one of the greatest crimes against our own people if we had fallen down under the threat of Mr Molotov ... I will submit to no threats from anyone.
>
> There is no basis for disarmament and for confidence until you can get the nations of the world to commit themselves to collective security as a fundamental principle on which other things can be built. We must proceed to develop regional pacts of collective security where we can, and not wait for the final agreement of everybody.
>
> We were trying very hard to get currency reform for all the four zones, but suddenly the Soviet cancelled the Four-Power meeting. The three powers have gone on and are preparing their plans. Currency reform is absolutely essential if we are to get Germany going at all. But this quadripartite business has held it up so long.

The mood in Berlin was described as one of 'undisguised pessimism'. As the German Economic Council sat down to discuss the imminent currency reform on 15 June, West German politicians decried the lack of consideration of German views in the whole process. Whilst the date of the changeover was an official secret, prevalent speculation suggested Sunday, 20 June as the most likely.

Then on Sunday, 13 June, the Western authorities had to deal with the fallout of new Russian rules governing travel and the transport of goods into the Soviet zone. Travellers from the West had been turned away for several days already, but on that day the Russians 'arbitrarily

Red Army tanks pass the Reichstag, their nation's flag topping the building.

A high U.S. military government official said last night in Berlin that there is very strong evidence that German scientists are producing large quantities of mesothorium for one of the occupying forces here. Mesothorium is a radioactive metal used in nuclear fission and the manufacture of atomic bombs. U.S. forces were confiscating stocks of the metal being offered on the black market in Berlin. Quantities of mesothorium and of radium, together worth £250,000, were already in American hands after a police raid, the official said. Twenty Germans and a Dutchman were arrested. He indicated that Russia was the power for whom the metal was produced originally.

The Courier and Advertiser, 6 December 1947

and without notice' impounded in their zone eight trains from the British-American zones. The Russian authorities pointed out that new requirements had not been complied with: an itemised listing of contents, designation of the specific consignee, and of the unloading station. That night, after an intense day of negotiating with obstinate Soviet bureaucrats, the trains were released, but the incident proved to be a seminal event in the history of the Cold War.

The following week, while the British military governor, General Brian Robertson, was in Frankfurt discussing the implementation planning of the new currency with his American and French counterparts, the German population in the West were using up their marks on whatever they could. Ladies' hairdressers reported a massive upsurge in business. The black-market value of cigarettes doubled to 12 marks (6d.).

The Soviet response was unequivocal: 'This will necessarily lead to the incorporation of Berlin in the currency reform of the city's natural hinterland, the Soviet zone. The inclusion of Berlin in the Eastern zone will result in closer political and economic integration of the capital in the surrounding provinces of the Soviet zone.'

At 10 am on 15 June, the Elbe Bridge – the only Allied motor road to Berlin from the West – was closed by the Russians for 'repairs'. The next night, heavily guarded Allied convoys left the Reichsbank with the new currency.

On 18 June, three German tobacco experts met with British and American authorities to formulate a plan to break up the highly influential cigarette black market, without which financial stability would not be achieved. It was envisaged that up to £3 million would be spent on the purchase of between 10,000 and 50,000 tons of raw American tobacco to be manufactured into cigarettes by German factories.

That same day, the Soviet military commander in Germany, Marshal Vasily Sokolovsky, issued an order, effective at midnight, banning all road and rail traffic from Western Germany entering the Soviet zone. Importation of both the old and new Western currencies would also be prohibited. Sokolovsky, in his declaration stated, that 'the separate currency reform completes the splitting of Germany. It is a breach of the Potsdam decisions and the control mechanism for Germany, which envisaged the treatment of Germany as an economic whole. The Soviet representatives took every possible opportunity of reaching agreement on a common currency reform'.

Soviet troops with fixed bayonets immediately cordoned off the streets around the German-language Soviet newspaper, and reports were coming through of a concentration of Soviet tanks and armoured cars on the Russian-American zone boundary.

Left: Cigarettes in Britain were freely available at a fraction of the black-market price in Berlin.

Below: The final press conference at Potsdam; Roosevelt and Churchill are no longer players in the game. Seated L–R: British prime minister and successor to Churchill, Clement Attlee, American president Harry S. Truman, successor to the late Roosevelt; and the Russian leader, Joseph Stalin. Standing L–R: Fleet Admiral William Daniel Leahy, the highest-ranked United States military officer, British Foreign Secretary Ernest Bevan, American Secretary of State James Francis Byrnes, Soviet Foreign Minister Vyacheslav Mikhailovich Molotov.

3. HIGH-STAKES GAMESMANSHIP

Three scant years after the global conflagration, the streets of Britain and the daily lives of her people still bore painful testimony to the devastation that a foreign foe had inflicted on the island nation. Developments in Germany, and the renewed threat that this harboured to Britain's hard-won victory over Adolf Hitler, therefore, caused concern across the political spectrum.

Addressing Bristol West constituents in June 1948, Conservative MP Colonel Oliver Stanley assured Labour Foreign Secretary Ernest Bevin of his party's full support to 'defend our rights in the critical situation in Berlin'. He contended that to surrender Britain's rights in Germany would not only result in evacuation, but also a 'loss of faith in our power, which might prove fatal to our influences, and those of America throughout Europe'. Stanley was of the opinion that there was a possible connection between the crisis in Berlin and the crippling strike at London Docks.

The erstwhile British war prime minister Winston Churchill, though usually vociferous about Britain's Socialist government of the day, believed that the 'grave' situation in Berlin precluded the making of 'party capital' during the crisis. Throwing his political weight behind the Clement Attlee government, the cigar-puffing war icon stressed the imperative of a unified and strong stand against Soviet plans to evict the Western allies from Berlin. The *Sunderland Daily Echo and Shipping Gazette* editor gave commentary that was more succinct:

Leaders of the Four-Power Allied Control Council in Berlin: L–R Field Marshal Bernard Montgomery, Marshal Georgy Zhukov, General Dwight Eisenhower, General Marie-Pierre Kœnig.

The position is dangerous and there is no use in blinking the fact. We are back to the days of Munich again. We can only hope that we are able to present a firmer front, with stronger backing, than was presented to Hitler ten years ago. The big difference is that the Americans are in this, as they were not in the Munich affair. It is hardly credible that the British Government would make firm declarations about staying in Berlin, in face of the Russian attempts to get us out, unless it was certain the United States Government is actually firm in its intention to stay.

We must all realise that to make this stand may result in war. We certainly do not want war: the idea is abhorrent to all of us. There will be no war forced on Soviet Russia by Britain, France and America. There will be no war at all unless Russia wishes it, and only then if she has prepared for it and is ready to strike. If we abandon Berlin under Soviet threats and pressure, we hasten a situation which will make war even more certain.

To stay in Berlin will be difficult. To clear out will be to abandon those Germans in the Western zones to Soviet tyranny to give the Communists a moral and material victory, which they will exploit, to the full. All Germany would quickly come under Russian sway and hope of any successful resistance in the rest of Western Europe would evaporate. These may be the stakes for which Russia is playing in this game of move and counter-move in Berlin.

We cannot be sure, of course, but the time has come to tell Russia quite plainly where the Western allies stand, and to ask Moscow just what she means.

In spite of an earlier declaration from Moscow to the Allied military governments that the Four-Power government had to be restored as the 'only hope of restoring chaos', the commandant of the Russian sector reacted swiftly and concisely to Bevin's public statement. Britain and America would not be levered out of Germany: Russia formally refused to take any further part in the quadripartite administration of Berlin. This closing of the door was interpreted by the Allies as the Russians having no desire to debate issues of dissension, and in fact, a sign that they would fuel further chaos. A high-risk standoff situation had developed, in which any sign of Allied appeasement or weakness would immediately be exploited by Moscow with its own agenda.

There was also a somewhat naïve, prevalent train of thought that Stalin had no designs of plunging Europe into yet another war, but the strength of any such presumption was entirely made on the premise that the Soviets would win in the war of wills. The unpredictable, dangerous game of testing resolve of nerve had commenced. Joseph Stalin once said, 'Sincere diplomacy is no more possible than dry water or wooden iron.'

By the end of 1946, the European economies remained well below pre-war levels, dogged by ongoing food shortages and high rates of unemployment. Civil unrest was not uncommon. The situation was exacerbated by homelessness and an influx of millions of refugees from the east. Transport infrastructure struggled to recover from years of sustained aerial onslaught.

In January 1947, prompted by the US State Department expressing an imperative for the American superpower to adopt a doctrine of containment to halt the international expansion of Communism, President Harry S. Truman stepped up to the plate. America, the custodian of Western power and democracy, would not allow its international status to be usurped by the Soviet Union and the regimes it helped spawn in those nations to the east of the Iron Curtain. He immediately appointed retired General George Marshall as secretary of state, with the brief to formulate a master plan that would negate any designs Russia had on global hegemony.

Right: Churchill, dressed in the khaki drill of the colonel of the 4th Hussars, tours central Berlin.

Below: Nuremburg, the venue of Hitler's mass rallies.

In March of that year, the US president revealed his Truman Doctrine: to support free peoples of the world and to protect them from internal military subjugation or external intimidation. In a report from occupied Germany, erstwhile US President Herbert Hoover warned of the danger of the Morgenthau Plan clause to completely emasculate the conquered German nation: 'It cannot be done unless we exterminate or move 25 million people. The productivity of Europe cannot be restored without the restoration of Germany as a contributor to that productivity.'

On 5 June, in a key address to Harvard graduates, Marshall officially made public America's offer of aid to resuscitate the European economies. Moscow, however, was fearful of losing its iron grip over the Eastern Bloc nations. It would not allow Western scrutiny of their economies – a prerequisite of American aid. At the final session of the Three-Power (Britain, France and Russia) Conference in Paris on 2 July, which had been called to ratify the terms of the Marshall Plan, Russian Foreign Minister Molotov attacked the aid package.

In his official statement he contended that 'the tasks which are being set before this organisation or before the Steering Committee that the European countries would find themselves placed under control and would lose their former economic and national independence because it so pleases certain strong powers. The Soviet Government certainly cannot venture along this path and continue to support its proposals ...'

After Paris, Molotov's rhetoric started taking on unhidden belligerent tones. He accused the United States of being a 'fascising' power, the very centre of anti-Soviet agitation. The whole of Europe was invited to Paris on 12 July to thrash out the finer details of the implementation of the plan. Led by Poland, the Eastern Bloc countries refused to attend. After accepting the invitation, Czechoslovakian Foreign Minister Jan Masaryk was summoned to Moscow where a dissatisfied Stalin 'persuaded' him not to attend.

Seen as a direct and confrontational response to the Marshall Plan, the Soviet Union hosted a meeting of nine European communist parties held in Poland. Moscow's message was unreserved: American Imperialism was dominating the international political stage, and communist parties in the West had to take on the struggle against Washington's presence in Europe, even resorting to sabotage to achieve their goals.

The individual needs voiced by each of the sixteen nations represented in Paris gave rise to intricate and extensive deliberations. The Benelux countries wished to retain traditional trading links with Germany, while Sweden made it very clear that it would not surrender its long-standing interaction with the Eastern Bloc nations. Britain presented a case for special treatment based on the greater sacrifices made during the European conflict.

With consensus eventually reached, the Paris meeting culminated in a communiqué to Washington expressing a need for $22 billion in reconstruction aid from the super-power benefactor. Congress, however, faced a strong Republican lobby opposed to such unprecedented government spending – the Right preferred isolationism. Former Vice President Henry A. Wallace maintained that the plan would prove divisive, increasing the growing chasm between East and West, and in doing so, making war a distinct reality.

The February 1948 Czechoslovak communist coup d'état – 'Victorious February' – proved to be a major bipartisan unifying factor in the American Congress. Within days, the American federal government's bicameral legislature approved the first Marshall Aid tranche of US$5 billion. Over the four years of the plan, $12.4 billion would be allocated.

Above: Heavily bombed town and bridge on the Rhine.

Right: A British war correspondent interviews female Russian soldier Feodora Bendenko on point duty at the Brandenburg Gate.

On 12 March, after having been alerted to subversive activities, the American Military Government (AMG) in Berlin announced that it had raided two district headquarters of the Russian-sponsored German Socialist Unity Party in the US sector. Officials of the American administration's public security branch seized leaflets which 'flagrantly libel' the American Military Government. Dr Franklin of the AMG's civil administration branch described their find as 'worse than Nazi literature'. The provocative publications, entitled *Gangsters at Work*, likened the AMG's activities in occupied Germany to that of the American prohibition and organised-crime gangster of the 1920s, Al Capone. To illustrate their propaganda, the leaflets carried images of bloody fingerprints. Unsurprisingly, the Soviet-controlled media accused America of undemocratic and terrorist activities.

Relationships between East and West in Germany, already strained over the Marshall Plan, worsened in the third week of March when Soviet representatives failed to attend a meeting of the Four-Power manpower directorate.

'Our ally, Great Britain, has suffered much and fought gallantly. During that fight she has produced some famous war leaders. I lift my glass now to the great Air Marshal Tedder [Arthur Tedder, Deputy Supreme Commander at Supreme Headquarters Allied Expeditionary Force for the Allied invasion of France], aide to the great General Eisenhower. Look around in Berlin and you'll agree with me that the Germans will remember for a long time his technical and operational skill. Let's drink to him to him and to continued success for the British nation. And to the continuing friendship between Great Britain and the Soviet Union. That friendship is necessary for the future of mankind.'

Soviet Marshal Georgy Zhukov proposing a toast at a function in Berlin.

The 5th Queen's Royal Regiment salute the dais during the first parade of the Four Powers on Charlottenburger Chausse, Berlin, on 7 September 1945.

Using its position as chairman of the Allied Control Council that month, the Russian authorities 'postponed indefinitely' all subcommittee meetings. While Red Army guards remained at their posts outside the council's headquarters, American military governor General Lucius Clay refused to be drawn into speculation by the press.

In a guarded statement, Clay said that it was too early to identify Soviet intentions in the council. He added that the quadripartite council had not achieved anything of consequence in the previous year, so the Russian absence would have no impact on decision-making. In spite of Marshal Sokolovsky's announcement two days earlier that the 'Control Council no longer exists', it was business as usual for the *Kommandatura*, the Allied body that controlled the city of Berlin.

In an interview with the Soviet-licensed newspaper, *Vorwaerts*, Sokolovsky's chief of staff, Lieutenant General Lukyanchenko, alluded to the need for closer checks on vehicular traffic from the West, ostensibly to stem the flow of 'starving refugees and criminal bands from the West'. It was a recognised fact, however, that the main arterial routes served as illegal conduits for those escaping to the West – a far greater number. Political and military commentators saw the threat as an act of gamesmanship by the Russians, a red herring to facilitate road blocks and control points on the autobahn and in border villages. Such 'measures' would, of course, increase the strength of Red Army troops close to the border. But most of all, the Russians would prove that they could unilaterally sever road and rail links with absolute impunity. At midnight on Wednesday, 31 March, the Russians introduced stringent new controls on all road and rail traffic entering Russian-occupied territory.

The AMG immediately reached the decision to resort to air transport to negate unacceptable levels of disruption in the flow of rail traffic at Russian border control points – the so-called

Marshal Zhukov takes the salute as goose-stepping Red Army troops march past the dais during the first parade of the Four Powers on Charlottenburger Chausse, Berlin, on 7 September 1945.

Russian 76-mm divisional gun M1942 (ZiS-3).

'air passages scheme'. While British chief of staff Major General Neville Brownjohn lodged a formal complaint with the Soviet authorities, the Americans cancelled the movement of all their military rail traffic in and out of Berlin.

Soviet military police, armed with submachine guns, set up checkpoints at the Brandenburg Gate – the principal entrance from the West onto the Unter den Linden into Russian-occupied Berlin – and other crossing points into the Soviet zone. Ironically, it was only traffic into West Berlin that was being stopped and checked. Soviet border guards were also bolstered at the British zone frontier post at Helmstedt, but the British authorities announced that they were not planning to emulate the American air-route substitute.

In a sinister turn of events, a British spokesman in Berlin announced that there had been 'an incident or two in recent weeks' where Soviet fighter aircraft – most likely a Yak-3 or 9 – had 'dived at and circled' British planes flying along the designated 20-mile-wide air corridor across the Russian zone to Berlin. The Americans reported similar incidents, but formal protests to the aggressors were met with terse denials.

The British repudiated talk that they were considering fighter escorts for their aircraft flying into the capital city. They had, however, introduced two C-47 Dakotas for transporting high-ranking British Control Commission personnel between Berlin and Bückeburg in the British zone. The French also started making plans to replace existing train services with air transport from Paris to Baden-Baden in the French sector.

Concerns grew in London, with the Foreign Office convening special meetings to assess developments in Berlin. The latest provocation, coming so soon after the Russians had walked out of the Allied Control Council, was seen by Britain as part of the Soviet war of nerves and attrition, aimed at undermining the Allies' will to remain in Germany. Britain remained resolute: 'This pressure will be resisted with the utmost firmness, and whatever may happen, Britain will remain in the city.'

On 5 April, a British European Airways Vickers Viking collided in mid-air over Berlin with a Yakovlev Yak-3 fighter of the Soviet air force. On a routine flight from London via Hamburg to RAF Gatow in the British zone, the four-crew, twin-engine Viking, a civilian derivative of the Vickers Wellington bomber, had been carrying ten passengers at the time. There were no survivors from either aircraft.

At around 2.30 pm that afternoon, as the Viking was levelling out for final descent, a Yak-3 approached from behind. Eyewitnesses testified that when the Viking had banked to port for its finals, the fighter dipped below the airliner before immediately climbing sharply. As the Yak rose, it clipped the Viking's port wing with its starboard wing. In the catastrophic outcome, both aircraft lost their colliding wings, causing the Viking to plummet to ground at Hahneburg in the Soviet zone, just over 2km from Gatow. Allied crash investigators concluded that the Soviet pilot had disobeyed both the basic rules of flying and the quadripartite rules governing Allied and Russian flying over Berlin.

Unity in war and peace pledged at the Moscow conference in October 1943.

EGYPTIANS DIVE-BOMB TEL AVIV

Egyptian Spitfires bombed and machine-gunned Tel Aviv, Palestine's Jewish port, three times today. The Jews claim that one of the attacking planes was shot down and its pilot captured.

Haganah [Jewish paramilitary organisation in the British Mandate of Palestine] reported today that the Arabs massacred the entire population of the Kfar Etzion settlement, south of Jerusalem.

King Abdullah fired the first shot as the Arab Legion crossed the Allenby Bridge from Transjordan to Palestine. Amid the wild cheers of Amman crowds, including several thousand unveiled Arab women, [a spokesman reported that] Abdullah's shot was traditional, for his father, King Hussein, fired the first shot in 1916 in the campaign launched by the Arabs, which liberated Arabia from the Ottomans and the Germans. His artillery had fired on several villages. Arab forces invaded the Holy Land from the north. Egyptian forces have already crossed the southern frontier, and bombed and shelled Jewish settlements.

An Arab spokesman said in Cairo today, 'The Zionists willed this war by invading a country very holy to the Arabs. The Arabs have accepted the challenge, and are convinced that this is a war of life and death – either we reach a decisive victory or die an honourable death.'

It was stated in London today that the British Government was not told beforehand of [American] President Truman's decision to grant *de facto* recognition to the newly proclaimed Jewish state. Britain has not yet considered the question of taking similar action.

Yorkshire Evening Post, Saturday, 15 May 1948

Immediately after the collision, RAF ambulances and fire engines were despatched from Gatow to the crash site. After a brief stay, however, the Russians told them to leave. Elements of the Red Army then established a cordon around the crashed Yak, which had come down on Heerenstrasse in the British zone. In yet a further standoff, the officer in command refused to heed the general-officer-commanding British troops, Major General Edwin Herbert's request for them to leave what was essentially British property. Compromise ultimately defused a tense, deteriorating situation: a single soldier from each side would stand guard over their own country's wrecks.

British military governor General Sir Brian Robinson immediately called on his Soviet counterpart, Marshal Vasily Sokolovsky, to protest in the strongest terms. The former appeared to accept the Russian's apology for an unintentional tragedy. British authorities, however, were not convinced, believing instead that the pilot had been acting under orders to fly in a deliberately provocative manner around Allied aircraft. In London, the Foreign Office took a 'very serious view' of the incident.

The next day, Britain's Eighth Army hero, now titled Field Marshal Viscount Bernard Montgomery, arrived in Berlin for dinner with Marshal Sokolovsky. Landing at RAF Gatow in his silver Dakota, unescorted by fighters, Montgomery casually steered the waiting media away from any suggestion that his was a diplomatic visit as Britain's emissary. Referring to Sokolovsky, Montgomery was reported to have said that he was 'looking forward to [meeting] ... a very old friend of mine'. During a two-hour meeting at Potsdam, the Russian general expressed regret for the air crash, assuring Montgomery that he had no plans to disrupt British air traffic over Berlin. Sokolovsky pledged to allow immediate British access to the bodies and luggage of the British victims. London went on to lodge a formal claim for full compensation from the Russians for the lives of the eleven Britons who had perished, and for the cost of the aircraft, freight and luggage.

In what can only be described as recklessly puerile behaviour, the Berlin Soviet-licensed daily *Nacht Express* invited its readers to participate in a 'poll' to predict when they believed the Allies would leave the city: before 1 July? Before 1 October? Or not at all? A footnote added that 'large portions of Berlin's population believe the Western Powers will leave Berlin if the Control Council ceases to work'.

Upping the anti-Allies vitriol, the Berlin chief of Soviet information, Colonel Sergei Tulpanov, on 3 May, manipulated his radio broadcast commemorating three years since the Red Army took Berlin. Proclaiming 'only we Russians are for peace ... your champions of democracy,' he openly accused the Allies of looting Berlin, adding that the recent imposition of Russian traffic restrictions had been just in time to stave off the exports of enormous quantities of German steel and manufactured goods. 'Tulip' – the moniker given him by some in the West – warned of 'difficulties and hardships' for Berlin's citizens if the Allies remained in Berlin, cutting it off from the rest of the Soviet Union.

By mid-May, unconfirmed reports suggested that Moscow had sent a new general to Berlin with the mandate to complete the division of East Germany from the West, and to 'manoeuvre' the Western allies out of Berlin.

Alarmingly, there was also talk of Russia banning Britain and America from using the airports in their zones: Gatow and Tempelhof. In the absence of a confirmation or denial from official Soviet sources, an American spokesman for US Civil Aviation Control reminded those who would care to listen that the Four-Power agreement enshrined a guarantee of unrestricted use of their respective airports.

The Russians, however, continued with their flagrant disdain of the Four-Power agreement. After demolishing the British aid station at Burg, Russian troops levelled the American autobahn aid station 40 miles from Berlin. The move by the Soviet authorities was in contravention of the agreement, and ignored the fact that the Americans had informed the Russians, when they vacated the station three weeks earlier, that they would reoccupy the site in the autumn. The stations had to be completely rebuilt.

Ostensibly to gauge the wishes of the Berlin citizenry, on 23 May the communist-dominated People's Congress launched a three-week referendum throughout the occupied city. In the Soviet sector, red flags and flowers decorated the streets and buildings where large posters urged Berlin to exercise its democratic rights by signing the referendum. The party had erected booths to facilitate people signing the referendum.

The response of the American and French military authorities was swift, sending a clear message that such activity would not be tolerated in their sectors. Amidst accusations from the Soviet-licensed German News Agency of American strong-arm tactics, US military police pulled down the booths at Schoeneberg Railway Station. Unlike their French and German partners, however, the British did not ban the collection of signatures, dismissing the Soviet-sponsored referendum as 'entirely superfluous'. The People's Congress campaign persisted, characterised by systematic door-to-door canvassing and truck-borne youth workers shouting 'No Marshall Aid!'

DD Duplex Drive tanks, nicknamed Donald Duck tanks, amphibious tanks developed by the British, seen here crossing the Rhine.

At the meeting of the Kommandatura on Wednesday 26 May, deliberations over the proposed constitution of British, American and French liaison officers to the Police Presidency became pointed and acrimonious. Russian deputy Colonel A. I. Yelizarov, acting in Kotikov's absence, said: 'The Soviet authorities have been placed in a position where they might have to take the necessary measures to liquidate the abnormal situation which has been caused.' British deputy Brigadier E. R. Benson responded, stating that there was no intention by the Allies to jeopardise 'peace and order in the Soviet sector', adding that the threat by Yelizarov to bar a British officer from entering a Four-Power-controlled building was 'a very serious matter'.

Capitalising on the tone of the debate, Benson challenged the Soviet deputy to comment on reports that his military authorities were inextricably involved with the ongoing referendum in the capital, describing the poll as 'ridiculous activity'. Berlin did want a unified capital and nation, yes, but under a democratic regime and not a totalitarian one. Yelizarov retaliated by accusing the Allies of police brutality, with guns and dogs being used to prevent the people of Berlin from exercising their rights. He accused the French of conducting a pogrom to silence Berliners in their sector from a democratic process.

Yelizarov's tirade increased in strength and momentum, his vociferous finger-pointing finding Winston Churchill in his sights, describing him as a 'warmonger ... the inspiration behind a European movement working against the Soviet Union, and directing preparations for a new war'.

On the night of 11 June, the Russians held up a British freight train at the Helmstedt frontier crossing, claiming that the contents of four wagons of military stores had not been

US TO BUILD BIGGEST CARRIER

The US House of Representatives Armed Services Sub-Committee yesterday in Washington unanimously approved a Bill permitting the US Navy to start building a 65,000-ton aircraft carrier, the largest ever built. It will take four years to construct.

The sub-committee recommended that the navy be allowed to stop work on thirteen ships so as to divert about £57,250,000 to build the proposed carrier and missile-launching vessels.

With a waterline of 1,030 feet, the carrier will cost about £31,250,000. It will be 20,000 tons more than the US carrier *Midway*, which is the largest afloat today, and will be ten feet longer than the ill-fated French liner *Normandie*. The new carrier will provide a floating runway of 1,090 feet by about 230 feet. Comparative figures for the *Midway* are 968 feet and 143 feet.

Northern Whig, Tuesday, 18 May 1948

[Construction of the USS *United States* was not completed, and plans to build another four of these so-called supercarriers were cancelled]

---

listed on the waybill. By the following morning, all rail traffic into the city had been stopped. Ignoring demands for the line to be reopened 'immediately', the Soviet authorities lamely gave unacceptable traffic congestion as the reason for the closure. The ban was lifted 24 hours later and 30 trains held up at the time started moving again.

In an unrelated game of tit for tat, the British military government disconnected the telephone lines of Soviet officials resident in the British sector. Only days previously, Western officials in the Soviet sector had their lines cut off.

On 14 May, the Russians closed the autobahn bridge across the Elbe near Magdeburg, the Soviet traffic authorities announcing the bridge would 'be closed for a long period for repair'.

Three days later, the entire Soviet delegation walked out of the Kommandatura, announcing that there would be no more meetings.

In the face of unpredictable east-west rail passenger traffic disruption, on 19 June the British introduced restrictions between Berlin and the Western zone.

At this critical juncture, the Soviet military government had now suspended all Allied passenger, military and civil rail traffic in and out of Berlin. The only route left for road freight was via a wholly inadequate vintage ferry across the Elbe, with restricted hours of operation. Inter-zonal passes were randomly checked and rejected for no apparent plausible reason. In response, the Allies had little choice but to augment air services to and from the isolated city.

All attempts by the Allied powers to introduce a unified currency had failed. The Soviet financial chief in Berlin, M. Maletin, voiced Moscow's contention that the West's currency reform was bound to be an economic failure, with 'disastrous consequences' for Berlin's population. Any attempt to introduce two separate currencies would be met by the Soviet military authorities with 'determined counter-measures'.

Generalfeldmarschall Wilhelm Keitel and Grand Admiral Karl Dönitz surrender to Montgomery, 3 May 1945.

London now stopped wives and families from joining their menfolk in Berlin; the risk was deemed too high. On the night of 25 June, Russian police opened fire on British press cars for failing to stop at a temporary barrier erected by the Russians at the Brandenburg Gate boundary between East and West. The driver and two agency reporters were arrested for 'anti-socialist activities'. Two days later, American military police arrested Soviet Military Governor Marshal Sokolovsky for speeding in the American sector.

Sokolovsky vented his anger at his occupation neighbours. In an acerbic missive to the Western commanders, he lambasted his erstwhile allies: 'Through your unilateral, illegal decision, taken without the knowledge and agreement of the Control Council, you have abolished the unity of currency and completed the splitting of Germany. The Soviet authorities had been forced to take urgent steps to protect the interests of the German people and the economy of the Soviet zone.'

British response to the Russian ban was immediate: ten armoured cars were deployed to the Soviet zone border, from where Russian soldiers and German policemen could be seen taking up positions in trenches along the demarcation line.

The controversial deutschemark had finally arrived, but its problematic birth brought with it the greatest humanitarian air rescue the world has ever seen.

Future American president Dwight 'Ike' Eisenhower in pensive mood in the ruins of Berlin.

4. FLIGHT OF THE GOONEY BIRD

An act of ruthless inhumanity unparalleled in the history of the world. It is grave not only for the people of Berlin, grave not only for the people of Germany; it is grave for the people of the world. The people of the world will condemn unhesitatingly this effort to gain political advantage by an attempt to starve a helpless population.

General Sir Brian Robertson

In a flurry of diplomatic urgency precipitated by the sudden Soviet closure of all Berlin's road, rail and water links with Berlin, American under-secretary for the army, William Draper, arrived in London on Monday, 28 June. Following emergency talks with British foreign secretary Ernest Bevan, Draper continued on to Berlin to assess the situation for himself. Meeting with the American and British military governors, generals Lucius Clay and Brian Robertson, top of the crisis agenda was the review of Anglo-American strategy in occupied Germany.

Of prime concern to the Western allies was the welfare of their garrisons in the beleaguered city. It was believed that the civilian population of Berlin had adequate provisions for three to four weeks, so initial priority would be given to their own men in uniform.

The Allies had right of access by air via three 20-mile-wide corridors with a ceiling of 10,000 feet. Triggering Operation *Knicker,* on 27 June the RAF flew C-47 Dakota Squadron Nos 53 and 77 from Waterbeach, Cambridgeshire, to the former Luftwaffe airbase at Wunstorf 22km west of Hanover. At 6.00 am the following morning, the first Dakota took off for Gatow,

Field Marshal Montgomery during a ceremony at the Brandenburg Gate on 12 July 1945, at which he bestowed Knight Grand Cross of the Order of the Bath on Marshal Zhukov (to the right of Montgomery) and the Knight Commander of the Order of the Bath on Marshal Rokossovsky (to Montgomery's left).

the British airfield in West Berlin. In the following 24 hours, 13 of these Second World War workhorses and Normandy stalwarts freighted 44 tons of food to the British forces in Berlin.

Arguably the most successful transporter ever built, the American Douglas Dakota DC-3 was first introduced in December 1935 as a civilian airliner. Powered by two Wright R-1820 Cyclone 9 engines, production of this variant ceased in 1942 after 607 had come off the assembly line in southern California. In December 1942, the military variant, the C-47 Skytrain, took to the skies for the first time. Designated 'Dakota' by the RAF, the C-47 earned the affectionate sobriquet 'Gooney Bird' in an apparent reference to an albatross. The Dakota's prevalent employment to deploy airborne troops, particularly for large-scale operations – C-47s dropped more than 50,000 paratroopers in the first few days of the Allied Normandy invasion – resulted in a far less flattering moniker: the 'Vomit Comet'.

The RAF's remaining six Dakota squadrons followed the first two to Wunstorf, but circumstances rapidly highlighted the inadequacy of the limited freight capacity of these aircraft. By early July, the first of eight RAF Avro York squadrons joined the British airlift effort. On 5 July, two squadrons of Sunderland flying boats started to operate from the Elbe near Hamburg to Havel Lake in Berlin.

With the sharp increase in demand, it became necessary to contract civilian charter companies to augment air capacity, including three Lancastrian fuel tankers. At the end of July, the RAF Dakotas were moved to Fassberg, and a month later to Lübeck.

In August, United States Air Force (USAF) transferred its overseas Douglas C-54 squadrons to Fassberg in the British zone, a prelude to the commencement of further operations in December from Celle. The USAF also conducted a substantial airlift programme from Rhein-Main Frankfurt and Wiesbaden in the American zone. Codenamed Operation *Vittles*, the Americans mainly flew C-47s, which were later replaced with the four-engine C-54.

Their principal destination was Tempelhof in Berlin. In November 1948, the Americans completed the construction of a new airfield at Tegel in Berlin's French sector.

In the period from September to October, ten aircrews from the Royal Australian Air Force (RAAF), ten from the South African Air Force (SAAF), and three from the Royal New Zealand Air Force (RNZAF) were stationed at Lübeck in support of the Dakota operations.

Moscow lifted the blockade on 12 May 1949, but relief operations by air would only cease on 6 October, ending a humanitarian airlift of Biblical proportions.

In the latter half of June 1948, American commercial airline planes started making two daily flights from Frankfurt to Britain with cargoes forming part of £15 million worth of Nazi-looted gold bars and coins, to be melted down and distributed as reparations.

The gold, ranging from 300-year-old Spanish gold doubloons to the melted-down gold tooth fillings of murdered concentration camp inmates, had been stored in the foreign repository vaults of the American-operated Reichsbank at Frankfurt.

Established as looted by the Nazis from their victims during the Hitler regime, the gold will, after melting down, be re-allocated to claimant nations by a tripartite commission for reparations in London.

Torbay Express and South Devon Echo

Allied bomb damage to the transport infrastructure in some areas of Nazi Germany was considerable.

On 28 June 1948, however, and with the Iron Curtain resolutely in place between East and West, few would have contemplated the logistical magnitude that lay ahead. On this day, a *Western Daily Press* correspondent reported,

> Today, more than 100 US Air Force planes, with vital stores, will blockade-run in the biggest airlift operation since the war; every available American transport aircraft in Europe, and even Cyprus, having been marshalled.
>
> To fight Berlin's 'currency war', food and power blockade by Russia, British and American troops and civilians there [Berlin] will from tomorrow live under a tight austerity regime.
>
> Major General E.O. Herbert, the British commandant, yesterday announced these economies: clubs to serve only 'utility' meals; no more matinees at cinemas; bus services cut; all unnecessary lightbulbs removed.
>
> There is no immediate supplies shortage, but stocks can only be replenished by air.
>
> The German population is looking to the Western Allies for decisive assurances that they intend maintaining their position as joint occupiers.

On 30 June, almost 100 RAF aircraft 'crammed with food for Western Berlin' arrived in the besieged city, joining Operation *Victual* initiated by the Americans three days earlier. Described by the British press as the biggest British air operation since Burma, Foreign Secretary Ernest

A member of a South African Air Force aircrew.

Bevin and his American counterpart, George Marshall, issued a joint 'no surrender' declaration to their respective houses of assembly on the Berlin emergency. Paris, though less public, announced the country's readiness to assist the Allies to break the Soviet chokehold.

Between midnight and late afternoon that day, 116 USAF Douglas C-47 Skytrains flew into Berlin. At the rate of one every five minutes, this icon of Guadalcanal, New Guinea and Burma delivered 290 tons from the American base at Frankfurt am Main.

Logistics planners with the RAF targeted employing 200 aircraft by the end of the first week in July, thereby establishing an air bridge significantly larger than that of the Americans to the north. Consideration was also being given to a combined Anglo-American relief air-bridge operation, in which 360 aircraft would land in Berlin in any 24-hour period – a staggering one-every-four-minutes, round-the-clock undertaking.

The need for pragmatism to overcome limitations was also recognised early on. In the absence of rail transport to freight bulk commodities such as potatoes and coal, only concentrated, high-nutrition food items would be carried. By definition therefore, this could only ever be a temporary, emergency measure. The authorities decided that food quotas in Berlin would have to be rationalised and scaled down. Ultimately, any semblance of a return to normal life for the hapless Berlin citizens would be wholly reliant on the Russian Military Government lifting its rail embargo.

The Allies, fully aware that it would be naïve to even for a moment entertain the belief that the Russians were now sitting back while congratulating themselves on a job well done, repeatedly warned their pilots to guard against complacency and be permanently on the lookout for barrage balloons or Russian Yak fighter aircraft.

By far the biggest challenge facing the Allies was how to deliver coal into Berlin. For the 2.5 million Berliners, this fuel was as necessary as food to sustain life. Airfreighting was at first deemed not to be an option. As part of a feasibility study, USAF aircraft were conducting aerial surveys to identify suitable spots for the delivery of coal by parachute or glider.

King George VI inspecting Royal Air Force crews.

The airlift, meanwhile, continued unabated, growing in scale and momentum as the British and Americans allocated more and more resources to the exercise. Fully laden aircraft were now crossing the Atlantic from America directly to Berlin.

RAF Air Commodore John Merer, commanding No. 46 Group, ordered additional squadrons from No. 38 and No. 47 groups to Germany, under the codename Operation *Carter Paterson*. Named after the British haulage firm – established in 1860 – *Carter Paterson* was replaced two weeks later by the much-expanded Operation *Plainfare*. In one 24-hour period, *Carter Paterson* had flown 480 tons of food into Berlin's Gatow airport. On the ground, two shifts had been introduced to expedite round-the-clock unloading, a task that the ground crews, mainly from the Royal Army Service Corps, accomplished in a remarkable four to five minutes.

HELICOPTER REACHES 124MPH

A new world helicopter speed record of 124.3mph, subject to official confirmation, was set up at White Waltham, near Maidenhead, Berks., today by Squadron Leader Basil Arkell, flying a Fairey Gyrodyne. Squadron Leader Arkell made his attempt on a course of three kilometres over the railway lines which adjoin White Waltham airfield. The official record for this type of machine is held by a German FW-61 helicopter, with a speed of 76.7 miles an hour, but an unofficial record of 114.6 miles an hour was established by the United States last year with an American Sikorsky R-5, military two-seater helicopter. [Only one Fairey Gyrodyne was ever built.]

Derby Daily Telegraph, 28 June 1948

Sikorsky R4B helicopters.

Flying along the 150-mile corridor non-stop night and day, the RAF pilots often had to contend with hazardous flying conditions of reduced visibility. The *Yorkshire Post* of 2 July quoted the Gatow airfield's commanding officer, Group Captain B. C. Yards, as having said, 'We shall go on operating no matter how bad the weather and bring in our aircraft, if necessary, with the use of ground-control approach apparatus.'

Perceived by many as a final effort to resolve the Berlin debacle, General Sir Brian Robertson, in a letter to Marshal Sokolovsky, demanded that the Soviet authorities immediately lift their blockade of road, rail and water traffic routes to and from Berlin. There was, however, an awareness among the Allies that the Kremlin would take a long time to reach any decision, let alone offer a response, but Robertson was fully cognisant of the importance of diplomatic protocol:

My dear Marshal Sokolovsky

I note with satisfaction that the limitations which you had imposed on the movement of the German population across the border of the Soviet zone were temporary measures to protect the currency position in your zone until you had effected your own currency conversion.

I am glad that you have given orders to permit Germans with inter-zonal passes to enter and leave your zone as hitherto.

I note that you are doing everything possible to remove the technical difficulties which are preventing the movement of trains between Berlin and Helmstedt, and that you are confident that full movement of traffic on the line will be resumed before the supply position of Berlin becomes serious.

I should be glad to hear from you the date on which you estimate this will happen.

I must observe that barge traffic is not proceeding smoothly. I should be grateful if you would investigate this matter and give me an assurance that this important traffic will not be impeded.

In connection with movement on the autobahn Helmstedt to Berlin, you mention the currency situation in Berlin. I do not believe that you have any cause to fear that your currency will be exposed to any risk on this account, and I ask that movement of traffic on this route should be opened at once.

However, I would remind you that in my letter of June 26 I stated that I am willing to discuss the use of a single currency in Berlin under Four-Power control. This statement still holds good.

The first objective, however, must be the restoration of recognised movement facilities of all sorts between Berlin and the Western zones, and the resumption of the free flow of trade, thus enabling the people of Berlin to be adequately sustained in the normal way.

In order to facilitate this, I should be ready to meet with you forthwith to discuss times and methods of reopening communications.

Yours sincerely, B.H. Robertson.

At a meeting of the four military governors the following day, Sokolovsky was unable to give Robertson any of the assurances he had sought in his letter to the Soviet general. In anticipation of stepping up diplomatic exchanges, the Allies drafted a letter of protest to the Kremlin. The Western Powers took a deep breath and assessed a situation for which there appeared to be no immediate resolution.

Joseph Stalin.

Food stocks were sufficient for only three weeks, and it was felt at best that replenishment by air was not sustainable beyond another three to four weeks – good weather permitting. A shortage of coal would result in major disruptions to water supplies and sewage disposal. This scenario, compounded by a collapsed transport system, no electricity and factories remaining shut, might precipitate a flood of Berliners into the Soviet zone, and with it, the fall of West Berlin to Russian communism.

It was suggested by Western commentators that the Russians were hoping for such an exodus, as they would then win the 'war' without firing a single shot – Berlin would become theirs by circumstance. It was also plain to see that Moscow had the military muscle on Berlin's doorstep to support Russia's position. Including non-combatant military personnel, American and British zonal forces numbered 2,500 each – the French had even fewer. The Russians had very few soldiers in the city itself, but in East Germany alone there were 200,000 well-trained troops, many of them battle-hardened veterans of the Russian Second World War campaigns in Poland and Germany. There were a further 400,000 troops in the Ukraine, Poland and Hungary. The stark reality was that Moscow

Soviet troops file past a line of their tanks.

could swamp Berlin within hours of mobilising these armies, the ground forces supported by a substantial air force.

On 5 July, all leave for British troops in Berlin was cancelled 'indefinitely'.

At the same time, British airfreight capacity was enhanced by the arrival of five No. 230 Squadron, RAF, Short S.25 Sunderland flying boats on the Elbe near Hamburg. A further five of these enormous aircraft from Britain would follow, together with two transport variants, called Hythes. Landing on the River Havel adjacent to RAF Gatow, the Sunderlands were well-suited to transport salt as their airframes were already treated with anti-corrosion paint.

Fifty four-engine Avro York transporters also flew their first sorties, lining up over Berlin to land at Gatow with foodstuffs. Drawn from seven different RAF squadrons, this derivative of the Lancaster heavy bomber was a stalwart of Operation *Vittles*, the codename given to the Berlin airlift by the American military.

In spite of Allied misgivings about airlifting coal only days earlier, the American authorities allocated four of the cargo aircraft to dedicated shipping of coal into Berlin. Packed in 100lb sacks, the first delivery of coal arrived at Tempelhof on 7 July. For the moment, Britain decided that it would not emulate her American allies, concentrating instead on flying in food and flour. It was estimated that, if freighted in Dakotas, the shipping cost would amount to £15 per ton.

On 12 July, General Sir Brian Robertson arrived at the Foreign Office in London from Berlin to hold crisis talks about the rapidly deteriorating situation in the German capital. Moscow and the Soviet Military administration in Berlin remained tight-lipped, withholding any response

SKYMASTER – YORK COLLISION: 39 DIE

Sir Edward Gent, High Commissioner for Malaya, was one of 39 people killed when a RAF York transport and a Scandinavian Skymaster airliner collided in mid-air and crashed near Northolt Airport yesterday afternoon.

There were no survivors. It is the worst air disaster in British civil aviation history.

Sir Edward Gent was flying home for consultations with Mr A. Creech Jones, Colonial Secretary. It is understood he was to offer his resignation owing to differences over steps to be taken against Malayan troublemakers.

There were 25 passengers and a crew of seven in the Skymaster. Sir Edward Gent was the only passenger in the York, which had a crew of six.

Both planes burst into flames on striking the ground one and a half miles apart. The collision occurred shortly after 4pm almost immediately above the Mount Vernon Hospital, after the York had been circling Northolt Airport for an hour, unable to land because of poor visibility.

Pieces of both planes were strewn over ploughed fields and woods for almost two miles. The bodies were so charred as to be unrecognisable. A fireman said that everything had been shot into the nose of the plane. The bodies were found huddled together there.

Western Morning News, Monday, 5 July 1948

Avro York.

to Western demands for the blockade to be lifted. Instead, the Russians demanded that the Allies, in direct reference to the airlift, immediately cease their 'irregular' flights into Berlin.

The city's war-debilitated economy was on its knees. During the four weeks of the blockade, industrial production levels had fallen by between 40 and 80 percent, while some factories laid off three-quarters of their workforce. With the massive shortage of power, coal and raw materials, those employees who were lucky enough to have retained their jobs were tasked with cleaning up and repairing war damage.

In an increasing war of words, the British-licensed *Sozialdemokrat* hit back at the belligerent Soviet-sponsored press by calling for 'plain talk' in any discussions with the Soviet administration in Berlin, as this would be 'the only means to prevent a third world war'. The editorial added that 'it should be made clear to Russia that in the event of her refusing to reopen the lines of communication between Berlin and the Western zones, the Western Powers will themselves reopen those communications'.

While Red Army paratroopers conducted another 'exercise' near RAF Gatow, the official Soviet newspaper in Berlin, *Taegliche Rundschau*, said that Soviet flight experts had recommended, in the interests of air safety, that it was time to 'regulate the problem of the air corridors which extend over a considerable area of the Soviet zone'. The paper accused the West of ignoring repeated demands by the Russian military government to adhere to fixed regulations governing safe flying. Western analysts viewed the veiled threat as being in anticipation of the Allies' rejection of Moscow's latest response to demands to lift the blockade. The Kremlin had proposed the convening of a Four-Power conference to discuss Germany as a whole.

In London, Prime Minister Attlee met with his cabinet for three hours to discuss the situation in Germany and to consider the Soviet reply. Foreign Secretary Bevin then briefed the king at Buckingham Palace. It was felt in certain circles that the time had arrived for Russia 'to be warned in the strongest possible terms that she is literally playing with fire'.

Soviet troops on exercises.

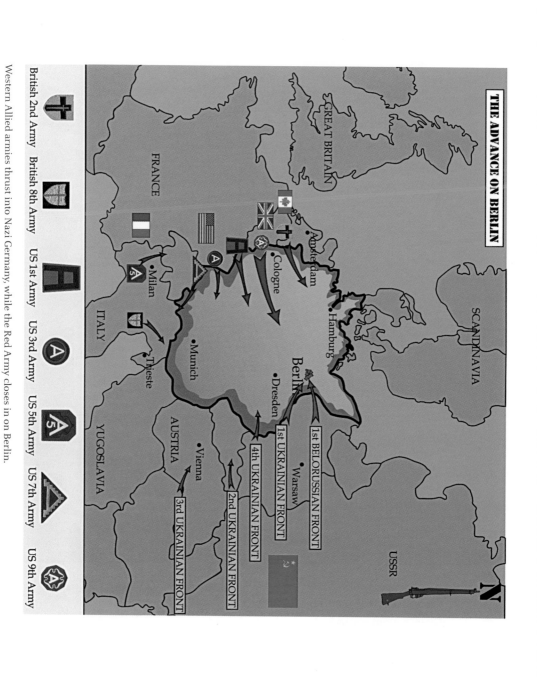

THE ADVANCE ON BERLIN

GREAT BRITAIN

FRANCE

SCANDINAVIA

•Amsterdam

•Cologne

•Hamburg

•Milan

ITALY

•Trieste

•Munich

Berlin

•Dresden

YUGOSLAVIA

AUSTRIA

•Vienna

•Warsaw

USSR

1st BELORUSSIAN FRONT

1st UKRAINIAN FRONT

4th UKRAINIAN FRONT

2nd UKRAINIAN FRONT

3rd UKRAINIAN FRONT

British 2nd Army   British 8th Army   US 1st Army   US 3rd Army   US 5th Army   US 7th Army   US 9th Army

Western Allied armies thrust into Nazi Germany, while the Red Army closes in on Berlin.

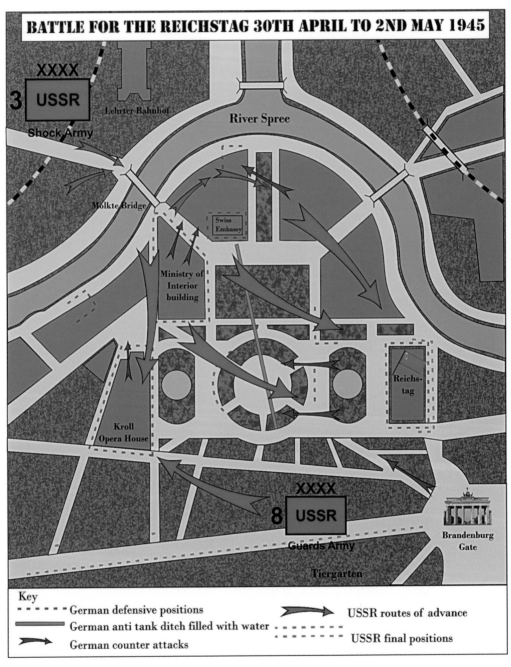

BATTLE FOR THE REICHSTAG 30TH APRIL TO 2ND MAY 1945

XXXX

3 USSR

Shock Army

Lehrter Bahnhof

River Spree

Molkte Bridge

Swiss Embassy

Ministry of Interior building

Kroll Opera House

Reichs-tag

XXXX

8 USSR

Guards Army

Brandenburg Gate

Tiergarten

Key

- - - - - German defensive positions

————— German anti tank ditch filled with water

→ German counter attacks

⟹ USSR routes of advance

· - · - · - · USSR final positions

The final stages of the Battle for Berlin as crack, battle-hardened Soviet troops envelope Hitler's citadel.

Occupied Germany 1948

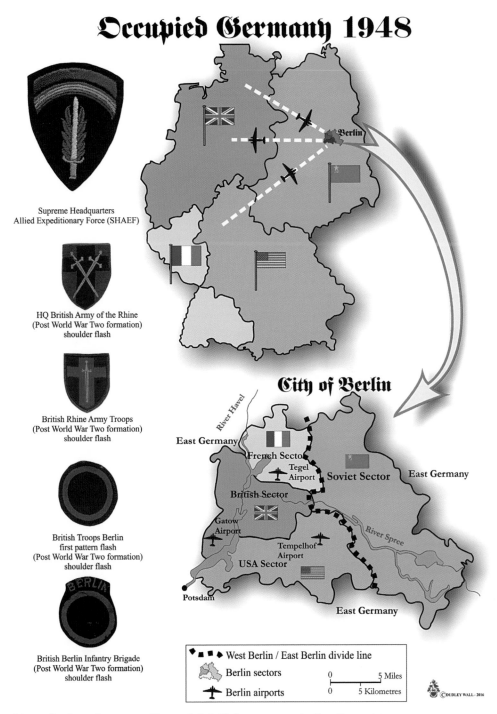

Supreme Headquarters
Allied Expeditionary Force (SHAEF)

HQ British Army of the Rhine
(Post World War Two formation)
shoulder flash

British Rhine Army Troops
(Post World War Two formation)
shoulder flash

British Troops Berlin
first pattern flash
(Post World War Two formation)
shoulder flash

British Berlin Infantry Brigade
(Post World War Two formation)
shoulder flash

Berlin

City of Berlin

River Havel

East Germany

French Sector

Tegel
Airport

Soviet Sector

East Germany

British Sector

Gatow
Airport

River Spree

Tempelhof
Airport

USA Sector

Potsdam

East Germany

◆■■▶ West Berlin / East Berlin divide line

Berlin sectors

Berlin airports

0   5 Miles

0   5 Kilometres

© DUDLEY WALL · 2016

The spoils of war: Germany and her capital divided out amongst the Four-Power victors.

AIRCRAFT OF THE BERLIN AIRLIFT

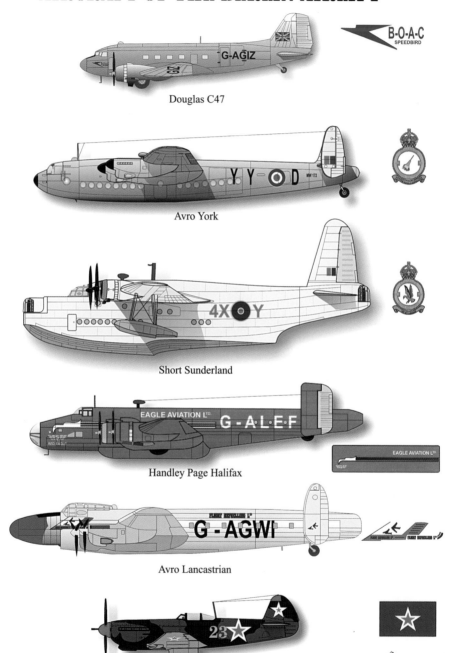

Douglas C47

Avro York

Short Sunderland

Handley Page Halifax

Avro Lancastrian

Yak 9 fighter aircraft

Some of the aircraft used in the airlift I.

AIRCRAFT OF THE BERLIN AIRLIFT

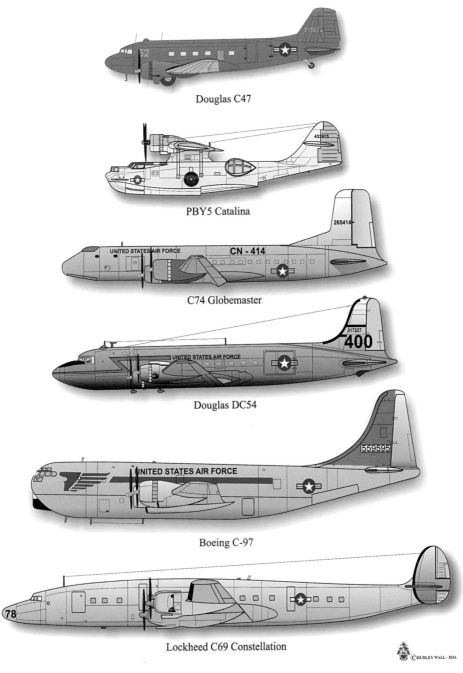

Douglas C47

PBY5 Catalina

C74 Globemaster

Douglas DC54

Boeing C-97

Lockheed C69 Constellation

© DUDLEY WALL - 2016

Some of the aircraft used in the airlift II.

USA INSIGNIA OF THE TIME

Supreme Headquarters
Allied Expeditionary Force (SHAEF)

3rd US Army
Deployed within the
US sector in the western half

7th Army
Deployed within the
US Sector in the eastern half

1st Infantry Division
Part of the US occupation
forces immediately after 1945

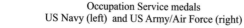

Occupation Service medals
US Navy (left) and US Army/Air Force (right)

Constabulary Europe
Part of the US occupation forces
comprising 10 cavalry regiments

US Army Air Force insignia

Cap insignia
enlisted personnel

US Air Force in UK

US Air Force
Air Transport Command flash

US Air Force
Troop Carrier flash

US 8th Air Force
flash

US Army Air Force specialist patches

Engineering   Communications   Weather   Photography   Armament

American insignia patches and occupation medals of the period.

COMMONWEALTH AIR FORCES INSIGNIA

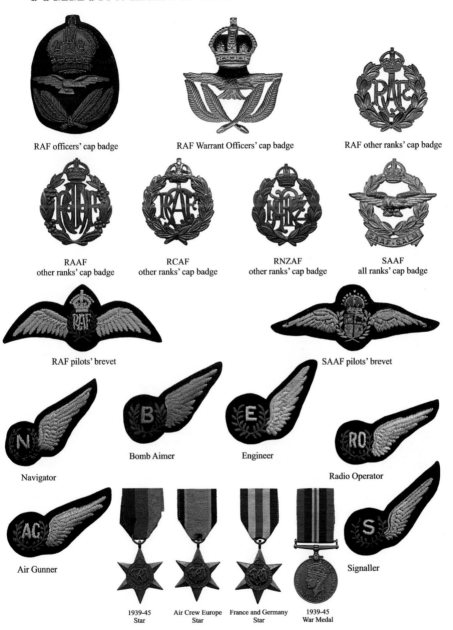

RAF officers' cap badge

RAF Warrant Officers' cap badge

RAF other ranks' cap badge

RAAF
other ranks' cap badge

RCAF
other ranks' cap badge

RNZAF
other ranks' cap badge

SAAF
all ranks' cap badge

RAF pilots' brevet

SAAF pilots' brevet

Navigator

Bomb Aimer

Engineer

Radio Operator

Air Gunner

1939-45
Star

Air Crew Europe
Star

France and Germany
Star

1939-45
War Medal

Signaller

Many of the British aircrews would have seen action over Europe during the war and would have been awarded the 1939-1945 Star, France and Germany Star, and 1939-1945 War Medal. Some would have been awarded the Air Crew Europe Star in lieu of the France and Germany Star.

© DUDLEY WALL - 2016

British and Commonwealth air forces insignia.

BRITISH ARMY GROUND FORCES INVOLVEMENT

Royal Army Service Corps
shoulder title

Royal Army Service Corps
shoulder title

Badge - Driver
internal combustion engine

Royal Army Service Corps
cap badge (other ranks)

Royal Army Service Corps
arm of service bar worn on the upper shoulder

Bedford OXD
World War II

Royal Army Service Corps
rank insignia - Crown

Royal Army Service Corps
rank insignia - Star

Bedford MWD
World War II

The Royal Army Service Corps was responsible for the unloading and distribution of all the supplies brought in by air to Berlin.

TYPICAL USSR INSIGNIA OF THE CAMPAIGN

USSR cap badge

Guards Unit
pocket badge

Order of the Red Star   Order of Glory (gallantry)   Victory over Germany Medal   Order of the Patriotic Front

SOUTH AFRICAN AIR FORCE INVOLVEMENT

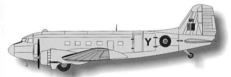

Douglas C47B Dakota flown by SAAF personnel

©DUDLEY WALL - 2016

Various players of the blockade.

The British press reported on Friday, 16 July that reliable sources had disclosed the content of a meeting of Berlin's communist leaders, in which a Russian political officer informed his audience that Russia had to grasp total control of the capital at the earliest possible moment. Equating the importance of Berlin to the Soviet Union as control of the Dardanelles and the Balkans, the officer revealed that plans to drive the Western allies out of Berlin within eight weeks. An integral element of that process would be to close two of the three air corridors, and force down any Allied aircraft flying along them. Marshal Sokolovsky had recently returned from Moscow, where Stalin issued new, strict instructions that had to be followed to the letter.

In preparation for the imminent Russian clamp down on the use of the airspace over the German capital, it was reported that the head of the Soviet air branch in Germany, General Alexandrov, had submitted comprehensive proposals to Moscow detailing measures that would give the Russians full control over Berlin's air corridors. Upon the closure of two of the corridors, the width of the one remaining would be reduced from 30 miles to ten. In addition, every single aircraft plying this corridor would require permission from the Soviet authorities before undertaking the flight. Such requests would have to accompanied by detailed bills of lading and passenger lists if they were to be carried. Aircraft flying without Russian authorisation would be brought down. Sources reported that anti-aircraft units in the western area of Russian Germany between the West's zones and Berlin had been significantly strengthened in the last few weeks.

Across the Atlantic, in another show of his uncompromising abhorrence of Communism, and therefore personal interest in the Berlin crisis, American President Truman flexed his nation's superpower muscle. Contributing again to what became regarded as one of his greatest foreign policy successes, Truman, upon hearing of Russian designs to close two

Above left: Soviet 61-K 37mm anti-aircraft gun.

Above right: B-29s parked up in the US zone near Munich.

of the Allied air corridors, immediately ordered a first wave of six squadrons of 60 Boeing B-29 Superfortress bombers to England. With these bombing groups to be based at RAF stations Scampton, Waddington and Marham in Lincolnshire, Truman ordered further B-29s to Germany.

The British Air Ministry announced that the movement of aircraft from the United States was only for 'a short period of temporary duty ... part of the normal long-range flight training programme instituted more than a year ago'. Included in the trans-Atlantic air deployment were Douglas C-54 Skymaster transporters carrying supplies, ground crew and maintenance personnel.

History will never forget the name *Enola Gay*, the Boeing B-29 Superfortress that became the first aircraft to drop an atomic bomb, and that in anger. On 6 August 1945, Pilot Colonel Paul Tibbets flew the bomber over a barely awake, unsuspecting Hiroshima, where he released the 9,700lb 'Little Boy' atomic bomb, vaporising an estimated 70,000 Japanese in the ensuing catastrophic inferno. Perhaps the irony that it was the same Truman who had introduced the world to the apocalyptic mass destruction of human beings, and who was now ordering Superfortresses to Stalin's doorstep, would not be lost on Moscow. The 'Silverplate' atomic-bomb-adapted B-29s would, however, only arrive in April 1949.

The newly formed US 3rd Air Division, headquartered at RAF Marham, Norfolk, commanded the B-29 operations in Britain. Flying in from their base at Rapid City, North Dakota, the B-29s of 28th Bombardment Group landed at RAF Scampton and RAF Waddington on 17 July, the majority of the 11-man crews veterans of Second World War campaigns in Europe. Painted silver on top and black underneath, the bombers sported a black R in a black circle on the tailfin, identifying the group and the parent unit, the 15th Air Force, respectively.

Speculation and rumours swept diplomatic circles. 'Reliable' sources confirmed that the Russian written plans that would bring about the closure of two of the three Allied air corridors were on their way to Moscow. The Americans were planning, after giving the Soviet military authorities due notice, to send an armed convoy of trucks along the autobahn to Berlin with instructions to employ force to breech Red Army roadblocks.

While the corridors in the Pentagon and the Kremlin were abuzz with a precarious game of 'call my bluff', relief operations continued to expand to meet the seemingly insatiable demand from the citizens of Berlin. A new 3,000-yard runway had been completed at Gatow Airport, which meant the much larger four-engine Yorks would join the Dakotas in round-the-clock flying of supplies into Berlin.

In a 24-hour period ending at 9.00 pm on Friday, 16 July, 207 British aircraft, including 109 Dakotas, 81 Yorks and 12 Sunderland flying boats, ferried supplies into Berlin. In about the same period, their American colleagues flew 260 sorties totalling 1,435 tons, bringing the American total since commencement of operations on 26 June to 16,660 tons.

With the potential knock-on effect of a looming coal shortage, the American, British and French military authorities ordered all food-manufacturing industries in the Western sectors to halt production, with the exception of those manufacturing margarine and bread. Traders and other consumers whose stocks of solid fuel exceeded a consumption of ten summer days would have their stocks sealed by the governments.

The announcement outlining the new emergency measures was made shortly after the British made public their intention to introduce 'Flying Coal Carts' into Berlin at the rate of six an hour. Amidst reports that the Americans were about to boost their relief airfreight capacity

A CUCKOO IN THE NEST

Analogies can be dangerous, but is not the position of Russia in Berlin hit off rather aptly by the picture in last night's Evening Post of an aggressive young cuckoo usurping a rightful brood in strange surroundings?

It is taking the West all its time, like these pied wagtail foster parents in Leeds, to fly in and keep a footing that is certainly legitimate. The pictured cuckoo might have been a cartoonist's impression of Sokolovsky, the Russian Military Governor, 'showing resentment at any intrusion with deft pecks'.

Let us remember the cuckoo's real parentage, and that he is migratory. He is 'thrutching' in the Berlin nest because it is his extraordinary nature. He comes from anywhere between the Ukraine and Vladivostok. And a Communist cuckoo behaves like its species.

If, in the European nest, it outrages our sense of fairness and decency, let us remember that the balance of nature, like the balance of power, is a constant equilibrium of forces perhaps irreconcilable in themselves. Moreover, cuckoo fledglings do not stay permanently in the nest, any more than the wagtails they try to oust.

This dangerous analogy can be pushed still further. The very nest itself is on someone else's property. The old car in which the wagtails built their nest is rather like derelict Berlin. The RAF laid an egg or two there. No wonder there is a mixed brood! But the point is that, like Omar's Sultans, we shall all quit the 'battered caravanserai' that is Berlin when the world eventually pulls itself together.

The crisis, on a long view, is a seasonal and local one. The German nation, now in the scrapyard with a vengeance, will be cleared up, be transformed, play its part again in the comity of nations. In the meantime, like the gallant Leeds wagtails, we must keep our tails up and continue to fly into a nest where we have natural rights. We must tolerate the 'deft pecks' without losing our tempers until such time as this monstrous bird matures and migrates. Looking well ahead we may even come to hear its adult voice without fear in a peaceful springtime as it 'shouts all day at nothing'. We must be as patient as nature herself.

Editorial commentary, *Yorkshire Evening Post*, Friday, 16 July 1948

British Overseas Airways Corporation (BOAC) Lancastrian airliner, converted from the British heavy bomber.

with an extra 70 four-engine Douglas C-54 Skymasters, British coal transporters started gathering at the British zone Fassberg airbase near Hanover, Lower Saxony.

In a 'fuel-after-flour'-dubbed flight rota, Dakotas from Wunstorf would drop off food in Berlin before switching to Fassberg on their return flight to load up with coal packed in canvas army duffle bags. The coal was shipped from the Ruhr to Hanover, where a German firm had been contracted to fill 250,000 of these kitbags supplied by the army. From here, the coal was trucked to a siding near the airfield. In a 24-hour period on 19–20 July, 202 British planes flew into Berlin with food and coal. Of this number, 76 Dakotas were dedicated to freighting coal.

Remaining aware of the German love for tobacco that fuelled a lucrative black market and collapsed the reichsmark, eight RAF Short Sunderland flying boats flew into Berlin with 20 million cigarettes. These would be distributed to the blockaded Western sectors on ration cards.

Determined to increase pressure on Allied airlift activities, the Soviet military authorities informed the Berlin Air Safety Centre that four groups of Russian Yakovlev Yak fighter aircraft and a group of Polikarpov PO-2 (NATO designated 'Mule') general-purpose biplanes would be flying in the air corridors on the evening of 19 July. An assurance was given that the Russian aircraft would adhere to air-safety protocols. The following day, however, British deputy military governor Major General Nevil Brownjohn was forced to lodge a strongly worded letter of protest with his Soviet counterpart, Lieutenant General Mikhail Dratvin, after a formation of Yaks flew over RAF Gatow at a height of 1,500 feet. This was in direct contravention of the air-safety regulations for greater Berlin, Brownjohn pointed out, warning that any incidents caused by further violations of this nature would result in the Soviet authorities being held responsible. It was believed that the Yaks had taken off from the neighbouring Russian base at Dallgow.

In Washington, Truman summoned his service chiefs to the Oval Office to discuss the worsening situation in Berlin. Talk in the State Department corridors was of a 'this is Munich' standoff. Washington, however, resolved not to emulate the naïve and gullible appeasement diplomacy of British premier Neville Chamberlain in 1938. The United States would face a showdown and all its consequences, including war with the Soviet Union.

In this unstable post-war period, when prime superpower status was being vied for, the Pentagon's short-term defence plans were based on intelligence conclusions that the Soviet Union would have its first functional atomic bomb in 1952. The crisis in Berlin provided few options: backing down was not one. In a three-point policy declaration, the US government declared that: 1. it will not be kicked out of Berlin, and will resist Soviet force with force; 2. it remained determined to resolve the situation peacefully through diplomatic channels; and 3. by exercising restraint in word and deed, leave the door open to any Russian approaches there may be seeking a peaceful settlement.

In Portsmouth, the British Home Fleet was mobilised after having been stood down in October the previous year. The 5,800-ton cruiser HMS *Sirius* had already left the naval base. The 35,000-ton HMS *Duke of York*, flagship of the commander of the Home Fleet, Vice Admiral Sir Rhoderick McGrigor, and light-fleet aircraft carrier HMS *Theseus* (13,500 tons), flagship of Rear Admiral H. J. Hansergh, commanding the Third Aircraft Carrier Squadron, conducted replenishment trials at sea before setting off for what was described as their autumn cruise. The replenishment ship HMS *Bulawayo* would refuel both ships by day and by night, at low and high speeds. A Royal Navy spokesman at Portsmouth stated that all the extreme circumstances likely to be encountered in wartime and blackout conditions would be simulated.

Right: Soviet ground
crew service a Yakovlev
Yak fighter.

Below: Russian anti-aircraft
crews on an armoured train.

Considerably closer to the Berlin time bomb, work commenced on a broad plan for the defence of Western Europe in the now very possible event of war. The foreign secretaries of Britain, France, Belgium and the Netherlands, together with the prime minister of Luxembourg, met in closed session for four hours at The Hague on Tuesday, 20 July. Consensus at the meeting was of a 'grave' international situation, and one that France believed could only be addressed in renewed Four-Power talks.

In Berlin, the predicament was no less tense. British and American military governors General Sir Brian Robertson and General Lucius Clay met for three hours, but released a joint communiqué shortly afterwards stating that 'the discussion did not include any aspect of the Berlin situation'. Attaching little plausibility to the Allies' statement, the city's rumour mill gained momentum. Prevalent among these was a growing belief that the Western allies, after a meeting the previous night with French military governor General Marie-Pierre Kœnig, were about to force their way into Berlin by both road and rail. Talk of armed food convoys and armoured trains, however, appeared to have been taken more seriously by the Russians, who dismantled 8 miles of rail track on the frontier between Magdeburg and the Helmstedt–Marienborn border checkpoint.

As the airlift neared the end of its first month of operations, the Sunderland flying boat air and ground crews had honed their turnaround to 50 minutes per flight. Executing 18 sorties a day from the Blohm and Voss flying boat base on the Elbe near Hamburg, upon landing back at base refuelling craft sped out from the jetty. Without leaving their aircraft the crew were handed boxes of food containing sandwiches, tea, tomatoes and 'iced cucumber' with which to refresh themselves, while troops of the 16th Parachute Brigade and Royal Army Services Corps Air Despatch Company filled the holds with supplies.

The Sunderland aircrews commenced flight preparations daily at 4.00 am, and finished flying for the day any time between 7.00 and 10.00 pm. This was then the time for the night maintenance personnel to ensure that the maximum number of aircraft remain airworthy. Leave was virtually unheard of, with one day off in four weeks being a common work regime.

SCHUMAN CABINET RESIGNS

The French government was last night defeated in a vote of confidence on the question of military estimates when a Socialist amendment was adopted by a majority of eighty-three votes. Shortly before the vote it had been officially announced that the seven Socialist ministers in Premier [Robert] Schuman's government had resigned.

The government's defeat was due not only to its abandonment by the Socialists, but because a good number of Conservatives and radicals abstained.

Mr Schuman left the assembly just before midnight accompanied by his ministers to hand his government's resignation to the President of the Republic, M. Vincent Auriol.

Throughout the day's debate the Socialist group showed no willingness to compromise on their decision to vote for a reduction of £14,000,000 in the current defence estimates. Mr Schuman had already stated that the government could not accept this reduction.

Northern Whig, Tuesday, 20 July 1948

Clearing Berlin's enormous war rubble became a routine task for the city's burghers.

A member of a Sunderland aircrew, Signaller Cook, confirmed that they did not leave their aircraft for the full duration of the shift. He told a correspondent, 'There are hundreds of aircraft flying to the capital. They are like flies around a jam pot and sometimes it is impossible to get in a wireless call to Gatow. The waveband is crammed.' He added that he had seen many Soviet fighter aircraft on airfields in the Soviet zone. Other crew members said they had never worked so hard, even during the war. In addition to food, the Sunderlands had ferried 'millions of cigarettes, tons of yeast and stacks of mark notes'.

In London, Prime Minister Attlee invited Viscount Bernard Montgomery, Admiral of the Fleet, Sir John Cunningham and the chief staff officer in the Ministry of Defence, Lieutenant General Sir Leslie Hollis, to attend a cabinet meeting. The agenda was not divulged, but Montgomery's presence added credence to unconfirmed reports that Britain and France were ready to provide America with naval and airbases in Europe. This was repudiated in informed circles, where the belief was that Attlee was pursuing diplomatic, face-saving solutions to the Berlin impasse. Timing would be fundamental in orchestrating a scenario where sufficient tact would allow the Soviet Union an opportunity to lift the blockade before a fresh Four-Power conference was convened.

In the House of Commons, wartime prime minister Winston Churchill remained obdurate, pushing Foreign Secretary Bevin to make a public statement addressing the importance of the military aspect of any resolution to the Berlin problem, 'for it is very important that the military aspect should not be out of line with the diplomatic procedure'. Unperturbed by shouts of 'warmonger' from the benches, Churchill merely paused, before asking if Bevin would like to make a statement on the issue, 'usefully next week'.

At the end of his visit to Washington, where he twice met with Truman and reported to Congress and the House of Representatives, America's military governor in Germany, General

A modified
Halifax
bomber with
an underbelly
freight boat.

Lucius Clay, announced that there was 'a very reasonable chance of reaching a solution in Berlin'. Speaking to the American press on the eve of his return to Berlin, he re-emphasised the American position: no one wants war, but America will not be brow beaten to withdraw her forces from Berlin. Clay added that he had been assured of more C-54 Skymasters that would almost double the daily freight into Berlin from 2,500 to 4,500 tons.

In Berlin, however, diplomatic sweet-talking continued to be overshadowed by the flexing of military muscle by all the antagonists.

On 24 July, 16 USAF Lockheed P-80 Shooting Star jet fighters arrived at the American airbase at Fürstenfeldbruck in Bavaria, near Munich. Landing at the former main Luftwaffe training base, the squadron from the 56th Fighter Group, led by Second World War ace Colonel David Schilling, flew via RAF Odiham in Hampshire, England. Codenamed Operation *Fox Able One*, the aircraft made several stops en route from the Selfridge Air National Guard Base in Michigan to Germany. Flying in aircraft capable of speeds in excess of 500mph, and working on 900-mile legs to facilitate refuelling, the flight took 9 hours and 20 minutes to reach Scotland.

In Berlin itself, Soviet aircraft continued to taunt the Allies with breaches of flying regulations in the British Berlin–Hamburg air corridor. Multi-role Tupolev TU-2 light bombers performed practice bombing runs near Kremin, north-west of the city, while Russian fighters conducted air-to-air firing exercises in the Perleberg area. Of particular concern was the fact that, for once, neither exercise had been reported to the Berlin Air Safety Centre.

On Saturday 24 July, the 10,000th aircraft of the airlift landed in Berlin.

In a fresh round of diplomatic initiatives from the West, envoys from Britain, France and America, on 2 August, called on Stalin at the Kremlin. It was hoped, after a two-hour meeting with the Soviet leader, that an agreement in principle might be reached that would pave the way for a Four-Power conference of foreign ministers to air differences and seek solutions to the crisis. Soviet foreign minister Molotov was also present.

Following the receipt of the British envoy Frank Roberts's report on their meeting in Moscow, London immediately summoned General Robertson from Berlin, while imposing a total news blackout on the meeting with Stalin.

A week later the 'curtain of secrecy' remained firmly in place, the only sign of any diplomatic activity the return of Roberts to Moscow with fresh instructions.

A taciturn Washington, however, released an 'unrelated' statement to an international media starved of anything newsworthy: 3,000 long-range bombers are 'in process of rapid mobilisation'. The Pentagon announced that the B-29s currently stationed in England would spearhead this enormous aerial force. In a detailed statement, a spokesman said that modernised Second World War B-29s, as well as brand-new variants, were being fitted with British-designed equipment to allow for in-flight refuelling. Pioneered by Sir Alan Cobham and the Royal Air Force, these groundbreaking modifications would give the American bombers a far greater range. The United States Air Force, at that juncture, had a total of 400 B-29s in actual front-line service, with a further 400 undergoing rapid re-equipping and placing into service. As fast as workshop facilities would allow, another 2,000 in good condition in storage would also be modernised and brought into service.

On 25 August, the three Western envoys were in ebullient mood as they left the Kremlin. Maintaining strict confidentiality, all that was divulged, according to Reuters in the Soviet capital, was that the envoys 'are understood to be extremely satisfied with the nature of a communication which Stalin made to them at their last meeting'. The nature of the communication was not disclosed. It was only said that it would receive 'the highest level attention by the Western powers'.

The following day, France's Berlin sector commander, General Ganeval, introduced a glimmer of hope when he announced that, as a consequence of recent discussions by

THOSE VERMIN

Health Minister [Aneurin Bevan], addressing a miners' rally at Durham today, said of his 'lower than vermin' speech: 'When I speak of Tories, I mean the small body of people who, whenever they have had the chance, have manipulated the political influence of the country for the benefit of the privileged few.'

In an attack on Mr Churchill, he said: 'I have been in trouble with the Tories. I shall always be in trouble with the Tories, and when one of our people is not in trouble with the Tories we should examine that very closely.

'Mr Churchill has the impudence to call me the Minister of Disease when every vital statistic shows we are better off than we were under the supervision of an aristocrat.

'These are the facts. I don't suppose the newspapers will take any notice of them. I daresay, as usual, they will take a few sentences out and keep repeating them week after week, and I challenge Mr Churchill to answer them.

'I like speaking plain English in these matters. It is no use speaking with a twisted tongue. Let us know the facts and where we are.'

'I may be ready to be polite 20 years from now, when we are able to look back on 25 years of Socialist government. Then, maybe, I won't have enough energy to be rude, but while we have the energy to be rude, let us be rude to the right people.'

Yorkshire Evening Post, Saturday, 24 July 1948

Left: BOAC Lancastrian.

Below: Stalin, Roosevelt and Churchill at the Teheran Conference in November 1943. Agreements made at these conferences with regard to Germany's post-war future were largely ignored by the Soviet leader.

Western envoys in Moscow, Stalin had sanctioned a quadripartite meeting of Berlin's military governors, the first since 3 July. Currency reform, the principal cause of the Soviet blockade, would be the main item on the agenda. Western commentators were not overly optimistic, however, contending that the onus was on Moscow to sort out the currency issue. Without a willingness to compromise, prevailing Soviet mindset would make any such forum an exercise in futility.

In an unquestionably Soviet-fuelled demonstration on 26 August, a mob of 10,000 flooded into Berlin's city hall, chanting anti-capitalist slogans as they overwhelmed a police line in front of the building situated in the Russian sector of the city. Addressing the crowd, the deputy chairman of the German Socialist Unity Party, Karl Litke, blamed the city's civil authorities of complicity with the Western allies as the cause of economic chaos in Berlin. To loud applause from the fired-up demonstrators, Litke demanded the immediate replacement of the city council with 'real socialists'. He called for the introduction of a Russian emergency relief programme in which the Soviet Union would be the exclusive source of succour for the whole of the troubled and divided Berlin.

The next day, around 800 demonstrators breached barricades sealing city hall, forcing Dr Suhr, chairman of the pro-Western city council, to suspend assembly meetings indefinitely. For the second day, members of the 'indignant Berlin working population' hoisted aloft banners, placards and red flags, baying at Litke to outline his master plan for an emergency supply programme.

On 31 August, the Four-Power military governors met behind closed doors in a bid to find a mutually acceptable compromise to the stalemate in Berlin. Simultaneously, Bonn hosted the first

A contemporary map delineating post-war 'ownership' of Poland, Germany and Berlin.

meeting of a German constituent assembly, its members having been democratically elected in the eleven West German states. Senior representatives of the three Western military governments were in attendance, where they observed the tabling of a draft constitution promulgating a bicameral legislature and directly elected parliament for a federation of German states.

As the round-table talks entered a sixth day, a communist mob invaded City Hall for a third time. Strains of the Internationale accompanied thousands of left-wing demonstrators as they swept orderlies and Soviet-sector German police aside to stream up the staircase to the council chamber. Three pressmen were hauled down the stairs and assaulted. After a tense night behind locked doors, British, American and French liaison officers found themselves and their Western-sector police wards besieged in City Hall. What was a cause for concern was the presence of armed Red Army troops and vehicles 'standing guard' outside. American liaison officer Major J. E. Davison let it be known that he and his allied colleagues would not leave the building until the Russians withdrew their men and equipment.

Inside it was reported that the trapped French liaison officer, Major Georges Razovitch, answered a telephone call to hear the caller tell him, 'The coffin you ordered, sir, will be at the City Hall within a few minutes.' Not heeding the French officer's protestations that he had not ordered a coffin, the caller continued, 'Never mind, I will send it all the same. You will be needing it soon.'

In London, the Foreign Office said they 'need hardly emphasise the seriousness with which the deterioration in Berlin, resulting from demonstrations organised by a party which polled only 20 per cent of the votes in the last Berlin city elections, is regarded here'.

In a terse progress report to London, General Sir Robertson stated that hopes for some form of resolution at the quadripartite governors' meeting had not been realised. He wrote of 'considerable difficulties, exacerbated by an unforeseen increase in tension in the city caused by Communists forcefully trying to seize political control in Berlin'.

Following an anxious night during which the deputy commandant of the American sector, Colonel William Babcock, was arrested by Russian military police outside City Hall, the Soviet authorities lifted the siege after receiving a protest from British military headquarters. During the hours of darkness, 500 Soviet-sponsored German police, assisted by Red Army military police, had surrounded City Hall, blocking all movement in and out of the building.

By the end of the week it was clear that the talks had reached a deadlock; the Russians were unwavering in their demands for unconditional control of Berlin currency. That Thursday, 9 September, in a move clearly stage-managed by the Western authorities in Berlin, around 5,000 Germans gathered in front of the Reichstag building to conduct an anti-communists demonstration. Municipal offices, post offices and factories closed early to allow employees to participate. By nightfall, this number had swollen to a staggering 250,000.

Congregating on the Platz der Republik, located in the Tiergarten directly in front of the bombed-out Reichstag building, elements from the crowd tore down the Russian flag from atop the Brandenburg Gate, which marked the boundary of the Russian sector. In the developing melee, an Eastern-sector policeman was shot and killed, and two more stoned to death.

The platz fell within a half-mile band of no-man's land, introduced the very next day to separate East from West. A very dangerous game of one-upmanship had now become ensconced in the city's daily life.

As the situation in Berlin spiralled out of control, talks in the city were abandoned, with little realistic chance of a settlement being reached to the 79-day-old Soviet blockade. Colonel Tulpanov, the Russian military government information chief in Berlin, chillingly threw down

'TERRIERS' NEW ROLE IN WAR

New Territorial Army wil have a dual role: as a fighting force and as a leading army of Civil Defence. This is revealed in plans just completed by the War Office.

A nationwide recruiting campaign, aimed at getting 150,000 volunteers in six months, will be launched on October 1. In the event of war, the new Territorial Army will be called upon to: man the great bulk of the anti-aircraft defences of the country; go overseas to reinforce ports and airfields; provide a field force with all modern technical units for service wherever it may be required; help the civilian service in the event of an attack by 'mass destruction weapons'.

Although this new Army will be built up on a framework of volunteers, from January 1950, it will include National Servicemen undergoing their six years' reserved service.

From the outset of any war, the Regular and Territorial units will be mobilised as one national army.

To carry out its new role, the TA will be composed of heavy and light AA and searchlight regiments, two armoured, six infantry, and one airborne division, and corps and administration units.

There will be the maximum help from the Regular Army to ensure that the training of the new TA is thorough. At the outbreak of war, it will go into action immediately, without further assistance from the Regular Army.

During the recruiting campaign, stress will be laid on the need for volunteers from ex-servicemen with war experience.

Urgently needed are men and women who served as officers, WOs and NCOs [during the war], who can become leaders and instructors.

Lincolnshire Echo, Wednesday, 1 September 1948

the gauntlet: 'Perhaps my words are not diplomatic, but I am no diplomat. The events of the last few days have forced us to simplify the language of politics. The mighty Soviet Army which smashed the Third Reich will also smash those who are trying to build up a Fourth Reich under the same principles.' He issued a stern warning that 'Anglo-American provocations' in Berlin and elsewhere were leading to rapid preparations for war.

By mid-September, Soviet observation balloons, according to United States Air Force pilots, were being encountered along the Allied air corridors on almost a daily basis. The American authorities said the balloons, tethered at a height of 4,000 feet, constituted a risk to airlift traffic. Further concern was expressed over the Red Army's ability to increase the height of their balloons on a whim.

Meanwhile, against a background of ongoing diplomatic activity at the American Embassy in Moscow, the British-licensed weekly *Montags Echo* offered commentary alleging that armed squads of uniformed Socialist Unity Party members were being sponsored by Russia to significantly bolster Eastern-sector police. Emulating the example used in Prague, armed shock troops, sourced from vulnerable factory workers in the East, were also being enlisted in growing numbers. The paper foresaw an increase in civil unrest fuelled by Berlin communists, who would seize any possible opportunity to physically vent their anger at the West. It finally warned of a communist putsch to overthrow Berlin's civil government, giving 7 November as a likely date.

At this time, the Americans increased their air capacity into the beleaguered Berlin, but at the same time increasing risks in the air, as both aircrews and those on the ground pushed themselves to the limit to sustain the round-the-clock air supply into the city. Mercifully, there had been very few incidents in the air, and those that had occurred were relatively minor. At 4.00 am on the morning of 14 September, while flying on the Frankfurt–Berlin air corridor, a United States Air Force C-47 Skytrain lost power in both engines. Flying from Wiesbaden airbase with a full load, the engine failures occurred 40 miles into Soviet territory. In his final communication with the tower in Frankfurt, the pilot radioed that his aircraft was losing height, forcing him and his co-pilot to bale out. The C-47 came down near Langensalza inside the Soviet zone. The Russians repatriated the two airmen the next day.

With each passing day, it became more and more apparent that diplomatic deliberations in Moscow between Molotov and the Western envoys would yet again end in deadlock.

80 TRIPS THROUGH BERLIN BLOCKADE

Flight Lieutenant Lionel Geekie, RAF Transport Command, is home in Dundee on a five-day break from the Berlin airlift. Captain of a four-engined York, he flies from Wunstorf, near Hanover, to Gatow, and has made 80 return trips.

He says the Germans have great faith in the airlift, which, for the RAF crews, is tougher in many ways than wartime ops. In good weather, Yorks, Dakotas and Skymasters land at Gatow at the rate of one a minute, providing a round-the-clock service. Most of the men are working a 15-hour day.

Flight Lieutenant Geekie has flown into Berlin with everything from baby food and coal to asphalt and motor cars. His average load is 17,000lbs.

The people around Wunstorf are eager to help beat the Berlin blockade, says Flight Lieutenant Geekie. They have come to him with loaves of black bread, which they can ill afford to lose, and begged him to take the bread to Berlin.

The record turnaround for a plane is 40 minutes. At Gatow the flight lieutenant has seen women unloading coal and swinging picks to keep the runways serviceable.

Out of Berlin one day, a stowaway was found aboard Flight Lieutenant Geekie's York. He was a student from Frankfurt who had gone to the capital to sit a final examination. It had taken him nine days to get to Berlin from Frankfurt. By plane he had hoped to be home in a day.

In a cabaret at Hanover one evening, Flight Lieutenant Geekie and his crew were invited to drink champagne with an unknown man. Nearly a dozen bottles appeared. The flyers insisted on meeting their host. He was an ex-Luftwaffe pilot, full of admiration for the work they were doing.

Flight Lieutenant Geekie is 35 and has been in the RAF since 1940. He has the DFC [Distinguished Flying Cross]. His home base is Abingdon, Berkshire.

Dundee Courier, Monday, 27 September 1948

All the while, the Western allies continued to reinforce their own embargo on traffic entering the Soviet zone from the west. Patrols were increased along the full length of the frontier to prevent any freight traffic from sneaking through on any one of a number of highways. The process starved the Russians of badly needed coal and steel from the Ruhr. The British deployed 100 extra district police at the Helmstedt border crossing, while bolstering each highway checkpoint from eight to 24 police.

In a development that was viewed with both interest and caution, Dr Johannes Stumm, president of the Berlin west-sector German police, received an awkward written request from elements of the Soviet sector police across the border. Signed by several unnamed officers, the missive was a desperate plea for help: 'While expressing our solidarity with you and your police force, we regret that we are unable to support it openly. We live in the Eastern sector of the city and we are afraid that if we continue to refuse to join the Socialist Unity (Communist) Party, our flats will be confiscated and our families terrorised. As you are no doubt aware, conditions here are impossible. We have been forbidden to read Western-licensed newspapers or listen to the American-controlled Berlin radio. We therefore seek your advice and protection.'

Conqueror of Nazi Berlin, Marshal Georgy Zhukov.

At the rock face, the Soviet Union harassment of her Western neighbours in Berlin was relentless. Be it the backseat fomenting Socialist radicalism or shameless, overt sabre rattling, the Russians persisted in daily activities designed to destabilise the Allies' tenure of West Berlin.

Towards the end of September, the Red Army staged anti-aircraft firing exercises in the Allied Bückeburg corridor that ran from Hanover in the British zone. The Russians said that firing should be expected at any level up to 35,000 feet in the Dolle area. In what had almost become routine, the Americans lodged a formal protest. Notwithstanding the fact that Allied aircraft operating the airlift did not fly above that altitude, the Americans pointed out that it was sheer folly to conduct such exercises in the heavily congested corridor. The only response from the Soviet authorities was to say that firing would only be suspended while the regular Russian flight to Paris was in the corridor.

American pilots were instructed to fly as far north of the Russian firing practice that was happening in the centre of the corridor, but still ensuring they remain within the corridor limits. Even here, however, relief aircraft were being buzzed by Soviet Yak fighters. In one incident, a Yak came perilously close to an American airliner en route to Frankfurt with 30 passengers on board.

In a joint 'note' drawn up by the British, American and French foreign ministers to Moscow, the Soviet Union was informed that the Berlin issue was being referred to the United Nations for arbitration: 'The Soviet Government has thus taken upon itself alone the entire responsibility of creating a situation in which it is no longer possible in the present circumstances to have recourse to the methods of settlement provided by Article 23 of the UN Charter, and which situation constitutes a threat to international peace and security.'

Accusing the West of violating decisions contained in the Potsdam Agreement relating to a conquered Nazi Germany, Moscow countered by threatening to walk out of the UN Security Council if Berlin appeared on the agenda. Stalin was adamant that the only way forward was a return to the absolute functional authority of the defunct quadripartite government, in which would be vested control over a single German currency.

There was no middle ground. There would be no compromise. The Red Army were the ones who had destroyed Hitler in his very seat of power.

Berlin belonged to Moscow.

The first contingent of SAAF crew arrived in Banningborne, UK, on 26 September 1948 to assist with the Berlin Airlift. (Courtesy 'Porky' Rich)

The Operation *Plainfare* operations hangar at Lübeck airfield, just outside Hamburg in West Germany. (Courtesy 'Porky' Rich)

An RAF Short S.25 Sunderland discharging its cargo onto a river launch on the River Havel, near RAF Gatow, Berlin.

Vulnerable German children boarding a Short Sunderland for evacuation out of the isolated city.

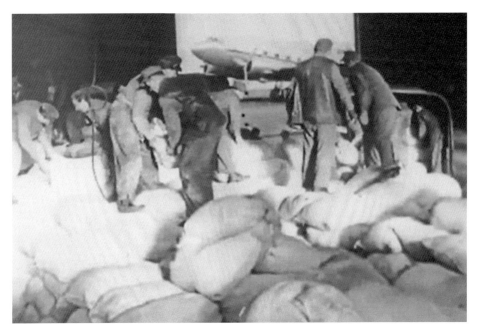

Bags of coal are carted out to a waiting Dakota.

Douglas D-54s stand nose to tail, ready to receive cargo for Berlin.

Handley Page Hastings in formation en route for service in the airlift.

A Handley Page Halton on the ground at RAF Gatow.

A Silver City Airways Bristol 170 freighter, its 'clamshell' nose doors open, taking on cargo for Berlin.

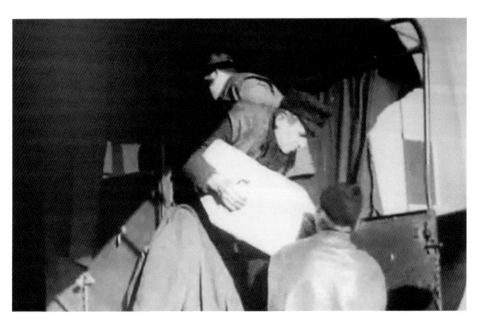

German civilians provided invaluable service loading and unloading trucks and aircraft.

An RAF Avro York on finals into RAF Gatow.

Congested skies and airport runways characterised the logistical nightmare that was the Berlin airlift.

5. COLD WINTER, COLD RELATIONS

As the trees in the German *haupstatdt*'s parks cloaked themselves in autumn hues, signalling the approaching winter, the breakdown in negotiations between East and West over the Berlin stalemate heralded an intensification of the Cold War. Covert diplomacy, however, now gave way to open diplomacy to stall the prospects of an all-out war breaking out.

The political focus shifted away from striving for a settlement between the two sparring parties in Berlin, to the global stage, where the objective was to drum up the greatest possible international support by each player. Success in such endeavours would place the stronger power in a position where it could confidently and securely outmanoeuvre its opponent to a point where they are forced to retreat. The diplomatic task of maintaining peace to avert ultimate war had failed, and with the threat of armed conflict growing once more, diplomatic efforts had to be centred on building coalitions.

Analysts now identified three distinctive scenes in this world drama. In Berlin, as winter drew nearer, the Russians intensified their pressure, while the Allies stepped up their airlift programme and the civilian population endeavoured to hold their own as best they could. In the wings of the military stage, the arms race was kick-started in earnest. Both power blocs knew they had to play for time: the Soviet Union to produce nuclear weapons and the United States to recreate a land force strong enough to defend Western Europe and the Middle East. Finally, in the centre of this game of power, the United Nations: the ideal instrument to nurture international support and to discredit the opponent. The Soviet Union knew that this was their weakest arena. Not only were they compelled to conform to rules and protocol, much of which clipped their wings, but to walk out would immediately result in the UN members closing ranks against them.

In the skies over Berlin and the Allied air corridors, the Russians continued to play their game of daring to see just how far they could test the West's levels of tolerance. In the closing

Hitler's war-damaged Reichstag in Berlin's Tiergarten, the centre of the city's black market; it would be ploughed for food production.

Victorious Red troops toting the mass-produced 7.62-mm PPSh-41 submachine guns.

days of September, American airlift authorities submitted a written protest to the Russian controller at the Berlin Air Safety Centre, charging that 'during the past several days, a number of Soviet aircraft have been operated in such a manner as to endanger United States aircraft engaged in airlift operations to and from Berlin'. The Russians were informed that two United States C-54 Skymaster pilots, approaching Berlin on 29 September, had reported that Soviet fighters had made 'tactical passes'. In one particular incident, five Yaks flew within 100 feet of one aircraft, while four Yaks buzzed the second C-54. The letter admonished the Russian authorities for failing to act on blatant acts of reckless flying by their fighter pilots. Wishfully, the author of the letter demanded an immediate cessation of such dangerous aerial provocation.

The greatest imponderable now facing those responsible for Berlin, and one which few had the courage to contemplate, loomed in the immediate future: would the capital be the darkest, coldest and hungriest city in Europe this winter? With typically phlegmatic Germanic resolve, the capital's citizens knew that they were powerless to do anything other than face the inevitable with strength and forbearance.

In the first three months of the airlift, British and American aircraft airfreighted 246,400 tons of supplies and solid fuel into Berlin. The Americans logged nearly 29,000 sorties and the British almost 21,000. To provide the civilians in the three Western sectors with a minimum of heating to endure the European winter, total combined airlift tonnages would have to be increased from 7,000 to 10,000 tons a day. At the time, the total haul of 2,300 tons of coal was barely adequate to sustain essential services. For each West Berlin family to keep one room reasonably heated during the winter months, they would require a coal ration of more than 900lb, which equates to an extra 1,500 tons a day, requiring 300 extra planeloads.

Even if such a substantial increase in coal freight could be achieved, generals Robertson and Clay were fully aware that there would be very little surplus for industry, and nothing at all for shops and places of entertainment such as cinemas and theatres. These would

MORRISON URGES RAPID CHANGE IN AFRICA

Mr Herbert Morrison, as Deputy Prime Minister, today opened in London the first conference of delegates from the Legislative Councils of British Africa.

He said that the need for adaptation by Africans to the post-war world was no less urgent than it was in Britain.

'A glance at Asia [Malayan Emergency] is enough to show the type of troubles which could break loose in your own continent if the right answers cannot be found and adopted much quicker than has ever before been thought possible. The good work which has been done and is going forward could still be wrecked by a failure to make big enough adjustments quickly enough. At the same time in this advance, which is part of the advance of democratic freedom, build firmly, for with freedom must go responsibility. It cannot be rushed. Move forward with the people.'

Mr R. [Roy] Welensky, a member of the Legislative Council of Northern Rhodesia, said, 'We will, I am sure, make full use of our right of criticism, but while we criticise we stand behind nobody in our loyalty to the United Kingdom.'

Sir Alfred Vincent, East Africa Central Assembly, said, 'Africa will become the greatest continent on this earth. But the work the British have done in Africa will never be forgotten, and the ties will never be broken.'

Dundee Evening Telegraph, Wednesday, 29 September 1948

German police and British military police raid Berlin's black market in the Tiergarten.

have to shut their doors the moment temperatures dropped to winter levels. This, however, would mean that entertainment would only be available in the Soviet sector.

The enormity of the situation, however, spawned ingenuity and innovation. A range of fuel substitutes and synthetic fuels started to appear in the markets. An example of one such mass-produced fuel standby was the 'Branda' slab. Made from compressed sawdust with an admixture of bitumen, the much-advertised product possessed considerable heating capacity. Thousands more, generally destitute, Berliners scoured the neighbouring forests collecting sticks, dead branches and tree stumps, which had to be dug out before the ground froze.

A soup kitchen run by the British military government in their sector.

Official announcements assured Berliners that, at present levels, food supplies would be sufficient for the winter. While the food would remain 'dull and monotonous', no one need die from hunger.

Although hamstrung by Russian dominance, the city council contributed as best it could. Apart from coordinating offers of aid from international welfare agencies and using its own funds, the council had stockpiled 14,000 tons of foodstuffs in Western Germany for the city's needy – the food only had to be transported to Berlin. The council also intended to have sufficient stocks to provide meals at schools, providing that the Allies were able to augment their logistical capacity to fly in extra coal. Without an allocation of food, the schools would have to close. The International Red Cross continued with the good work it performed for Allied prisoners of war during the war. Branches in Sweden, the United Kingdom and South Africa pledged assistance for the city's young and old during the winter.

Already on only three hours of electricity supply a day, usually just before dawn, there was talk that domestic gas and light supplies would have to be cut still further. Allied military and civil occupation personnel did not escape power and fuel restrictions. The Americans banned the use of heating before 1 November, while the British, who were generally more hardened to the rigours of winter at home, would introduce a later date. Messes were told that food supplies would be adequate, but 'very dull indeed'.

The fate of industry over the next few months remained an unknown. A daily minimum of 120 tons of raw materials would have to be flown in to avoid major unemployment, which in itself would not only add extra demand on the supply of fuel, but also open the door to civil unrest. This would provide the Russians with opportunities to further their own political designs on the city.

In the final analysis, however, the severity of the winter would be the largest determining factor influencing airlift strategies. The experts were understandably hesitant to make any confident forecast. The city had experienced a well-received warm autumn, especially after the cold and wet summer, a combination that had many an amateur pundit predicting a bitterly cold winter.

The Earl of Halifax puts his name to the UN Charter, June 1945.

On 4 October, the UN Security Council failed to commence discussions over what was described by US representative Philip C. Jessup as the Soviet Union's 'unlawful and hostile actions' in Berlin. The Soviet deputy foreign minister, Andrei Vyshinsky, challenged the legal right of the Western powers to table the Berlin issue at that forum. He stated that Russia would not be party to any debate concerning the German capital as it was in contravention of the UN Charter. The chances of the Russians walking out remained a distinct possibility.

The following day, subsequent to a nine-to-two-vote decision by the Security Council to place the Berlin crisis on its agenda, Vyshinsky reiterated the Soviet Union's contention that, by bringing the issue to the Security Council, Article 107 of the Charter was being violated. The future of Berlin, in terms of this clause, had to be settled by the Four Powers in council. With solemn voice, Vyshinsky ended with: 'Accordingly, the Soviet delegation will not participate in the discussion in the Security Council on the matter of Berlin.'

In Western Europe, however, the consolidation of what was, in essence, a military pact, was rapidly taking shape, recognising the need for a continental entity to assiduously study and find solutions to the tactical and technical issues facing a cohesive defence of Europe to the west of the iron curtain. To this end, Field Marshal Viscount Bernard Montgomery was appointed permanent military chairman of the newly established Defence Council of the Western Powers. A statement from the Foreign Office also divulged the names of senior officers appointed in terms of the Brussels Treaty: commander-in-chief land forces Western Europe, *General d'Armée* Jean de Lattre de Tassigny of France; commander-in-chief air forces Western Europe, Air Marshal Sir James Robb of Britain; and naval flag officer of Western Europe, Vice Admiral Robert Jaujard, also of France.

Welcoming the creation of a united military leadership in Western Europe, Washington said that it was 'one of the key moves before the United States can associate' itself with the defence union. Providing further endorsement, America pledged that, with the practical implementation of the infrastructure and functions of the union, she would support them with 'American arms and funds to make the alliance effective'.

In Berlin, the Soviet forces continued with their threatening displays of post-war military prowess. Russian paratroopers performed low-level jumps in the Hamburg–Berlin air corridor, with drops being made as low as 2,500 feet. In the space of 12 days, the Americans had logged 86 incidents of aerial harassment by fighters of the Soviet air force. British aircrews engaged in the airlift reported that they had witnessed Soviet aircraft dropping live bombs in their own zone, 12 miles north-west of Berlin. There was no denial from the Russian military government, only a belated notification that 'full-scale air-war manoeuvres' would be conducted by the Soviet air force in the Allied air corridors and over Berlin. The exercises notification, only received after they had commenced, would include heavy anti-aircraft firing, mass parachute jumps by the Red Army, air-to-air and ground-to-air firing, and formation flying.

An unnamed senior American officer in the capital estimated that there were now 4,500 Soviet aircraft in Germany, which included 1,600 front-line combat aircraft and a handful of the Russian variant of the Boeing B-29 Superfortress. Such an armada of aircraft outnumbered ten times that of the United States Air Force based in Germany.

Perhaps still basking in the hero status of a victorious wartime leader, the irrepressible Winston Churchill steamrolled his way into the diplomatic fray. With characteristically unveiled oratory, at the October Conservative Conference he lambasted the British Socialist government for the 'unskilful manner in which our foreign affairs have been handled', thereby

---

ACROSS WORLD IN AN HOUR BY PASSENGER ROCKET

Rocket projectiles bringing any point on the earth's surface with an hour's time of any other point, at an economic fare, is the ultimate peak of high-speed transport to which we can look forward.

Mr Peter G. Masefield, long-term planning director at the Ministry of Civil Aviation, presented the theory to the Royal Aeronautical Society in London last night.

'Ten to twelve years from now,' he said, 'air transport should have achieved a sound commercial basis without direct subsidy. Until aircraft can be landed safely on individual runways in all weathers at a rate of not less than thirty per hour, the full realisation of air transport cannot be achieved. Cheap fast air transport depends on the solution of the problems of air traffic control.'

The propeller-turbine is likely to show advantages over the piston engine for nearly all operations. The plain jet turbine will probably show improved commercial efficiency at supersonic speeds up to about 1,500mph at 75,000 feet. Rocket power plant should give commercial aircraft speeds of up to 5,000mph.

The commercial helicopter, in sizes of not less than ten seats, will find its most useful application in stages as from 50 to 200 miles, particularly for journeys involving short sea crossings. Helicopter development is likely to be rapid during the next ten years.

Dundee Courier, Friday, 1 October 1948

British troops and West Berlin police check a motorist's papers.

'creating the abyss which now yawns across Europe and the World. Nothing stands between Europe today and complete subjugation to Communist tyranny but the atomic bomb in American possession'. Churchill warned that the Soviet Union was now so heavily armed in Europe that her forces were considerably superior to all those of the Western nations on the continent. He asked, 'What will happen when they get the atomic bomb themselves and have accumulated a large store?'

And, in the face of an intransigent and obstructive Moscow, the West could only come to one conclusion: the Berlin blockade will only be lifted when Stalin says so – and only on his terms. He would exact a high price from his former wartime allies.

On 15 October, an announcement was made at Wiesbaden that the airlift operation would be merged into a combined Anglo-American force, titled the 'Combined Air Lift Task Force'. Major General William Tunner of the American Army Air Force would be director and British Air Commodore John Merer his deputy. The task force would have as its aim an amalgamation of effort: 'The delivery to Berlin in a safe and efficient manner of the maximum tonnage possible, consistent with the combined resources of equipment and personnel available.' The individual British and American command structures would be retained, with each remaining in their respective headquarters at Wiesbaden and Bückeburg.

Flight Lieutenant Theakston inspects a soap-making concern.

In conjunction with this development, President Truman assigned a further sixty-six four-engine aircraft to the airlift operation, as an assurance that Berlin would be well supplied during the winter months. This was to increase the total number of American aircraft solely committed to the airlift to 250. Targeting to have two-thirds of this number in service at any given time, it was estimated that daily freight transported would increase, in good weather, to 5,000 tons, which exceeds the minimum of 4,500 tons set to meet the city's minimum requirements.

On 25 October, the Soviet Union vetoed a Security Council resolution calling for the immediate lifting of the Berlin blockade.

In the divided city, Soviet military authorities ordered the only remaining railway line connecting its sector from that of the Americans to be torn up. Police posts along the shared boundaries would be strengthened and large forces of Red Army troops, armoured vehicles and heavy artillery deployed to the zonal frontier. Pilots along the air corridors observed that some 150 anti-aircraft guns had been moved into the air corridors. Long convoys of military vehicles and hardware were seen being deployed in forests and fields, including an estimated 400 heavy tanks and long-range guns.

Berlin's British military governor, General Sir Robertson, also accused the Russians of forming a 'formidable and distinctly military' police force in their sector, totalling 200,000. Stating that not only did this move break the Potsdam Agreement, but he also questioned why a police force should be armed with heavy machine guns, mortars and armoured cars.

Captain W. E. Birchenall inspects West Berlin German police in the British sector.

At the same time in Paris, following on from recent talks with Canada and the United States, the five foreign ministers of the so-called Western Union – Britain, France, Belgium, the Netherlands and Luxembourg – agreed in principle to the concept of a regional defence pact for the North Atlantic.

While East-West diplomatic relations remained chilled, at the end of October temperatures in the fuel-starved Berlin plummeted. Municipal authorities were forced to post night guards on the city's streets as Berliners, desperate for heating material, started tearing up the streets for the tar-soaked wooden blocks. The first domestic allocation of 20,000 tons of coal was announced, giving priority to the old, sick and young. In the British sector, the heating ban was lifted in staff homes and barracks, and offices.

With the arrival of the cold weather, in Germany the Royal Air Force's No. 47 Squadron, Transport Command, replaced their Handley Page Halifax A Mk 9s with eight Hastings, to be devoted to freighting coal into Berlin. By this time, the British and Americans had flown in almost 450,000 tons of relief into the city since the start of the embargo in June.

The drops in temperatures in early November, however, introduced the air traffic controller's worst nightmare: fog. As dense banks of fog blanketed the air corridors, pilots found themselves flying blind and having to rely on radar-controlled landings. The adverse result was a dramatic reduction in flight turnaround, with RAF Gatow struggling to land a flight every four minutes. The Americans exercised greater caution, closing their Tempelhof airport to all traffic on the first day of the month. The airlift came to a virtual standstill as landings at Gatow halved to 184 in the previous twenty-four hours.

GUNS BEFORE FREE SPECTACLES

In a plea for some form of national cooperation, Lord Elton told the House of Lords yesterday that the Government might find themselves compelled to consider not guns before butter, but guns before orange juice and free spectacles.

'We might well be within a week or two of the third world war, and still the common man clearly assumes nothing of the sort is likely to happen,' he declared.

Sooner or later the Government would find themselves following a course which would mean that their defence programme would necessitate a cessation of the expansion of our social services, and possibly even some reduction of them.

'I earnestly suggest that then Government accommodate their policy to the profound reality that, although we are not at war, we most certainly are not at peace. In every great factory, in every university, and at the head of some great unions are men and women devoted primarily to the interests of a foreign state, and prepared to play the role of a quisling [Quisling was the Norwegian wartime head of state who corroborated with the Nazis] in some way or other.'

Aberdeen Journal, Thursday, 28 October 1948

It was 18 hours before the 35 grounded American Skymasters could resume the airlift in two of the three corridors. The Soviet-licensed daily, *Taegliche Rundschau*, gloated: 'The planes are getting old, the pilots are getting cold feet.'

Logistics analysts sifting through flight- and control-tower data found reason for cautious optimism that the 'radar apparatus' at Gatow enabled aircraft to keep flying in all but the thickest fogs. The same could not be said, however, of ground-control approach landings. If the cloud ceiling dropped below 300 feet and pilot visibility was less than 500 feet, not even radar could assist the pilot.

Height and directions instructions conveyed by radio from the tower to the pilot could only bring the aircraft in close proximity to the airport. Finals then became the pilot's unaided responsibility. At that stage, the pilot was committed and must be able to see down the runway by himself. Fortunately, the early winter fog did not blot out those last few vital hundred yards, and 'radar achieved its greatest success since its invention'. The exhausted officers and NCOs boasted of their successes in keeping Gatow's 'delicate' radar apparatus operating for 48 hours without a break.

In spite of improved radar-assisted directional assistance, landings at Gatow still fell by 40 percent. The main reason for this was the grounding of the airlift workhorse, the Dakota, leaving the Skymasters and Yorks to do as best they could, even though their capacity was greater than the Dakota's 3 tons.

In poor-visibility conditions on the night of 17 November, an RAF Dakota crashed and burst into flames in the Soviet zone. Carrying freight from Berlin, the aircraft was preparing to land at Lübeck went it went down. The pilot perished in the inferno, which also totally destroyed the aircraft. The two crew members sustained serious injuries and were treated in a Soviet hospital.

In an avoidable tragedy a week later, the navigator of the above Dakota crash died from loss of blood in a Soviet hospital in a circus of deliberate procrastination by the Russians. After the

Above left: In November 1945, Marshal Zhukov unveiled the Red Army monument in the Tiergarten, Berlin.

Above right: Berlin women prepare soup in front of Brandenburg Gate before the cessation of hostilities.

twin-engine transporter came down on 17 November, RAF Gatow, in a war of words with the Soviet press in Berlin, stated that they had only been informed at 1.00 pm the following day that Flight Lieutenant J. E. Wilkins had requested a British doctor to perform life-saving surgery. The Russians suggested to the British medical officer to make his way to Karlshorst, from where he could drive by car to his patient in the hospital at Schoenberg – a distance of 150 miles. Objections by the British doctor over the proposed arrangements precipitated protracted negotiations in which critical time was lost. Ultimately, the Russians agreed that a British medical officer from Lübeck could be used instead. The distance was only a few wretched miles across the frontier, but by then Wilkins, whose home base was RAF Moreton Valence in Gloucestershire, had lost his battle for life.

A week later, as airlift personnel celebrated flight number 80,000 into Berlin, the city received its first snow of the winter. The record flight brought the total relief freight flown in since the blockade started in June to 360,000 tons.

In Paris, talks remained at deadlock, and in a decisive move with ramifications that would cement the city's political complexion for decades to come, Berlin's communist parties finalised the city's East-West split. They appointed their own provisional mayor, Herr Fritz Ebert, and named members of the council's administration. To coincide with this unilateral development, Berlin's Soviet-controlled radio station broadcast an appeal every ten minutes for the city's burghers to demonstrate against the existing *de jure* city administration that held its meetings in the British sector.

The 1948 festive season in Berlin was decidedly Dickensian. There was little to nurture Christmas cheer, the city packed with political Scrooges bent on widening the East-West divide. In response to the breakaway East Berlin city administration, local government administering the Western sectors held their own elections, against a flood of radio-based communist propaganda and incitement to violence by Socialist adherents.

It would have come as little surprise if a single Christmas tree of the 10,000 airlifted into Berlin ever reached a front room to be decorated with tinsel and baubles.

Fog continued to cause major disruption along the air corridors and at airports, reducing relief tonnages into the city. Notwithstanding the fact that, thankfully, it had been a relatively mild winter to date, demand for solid fuel still outstripped that which the Allies were able to fly in under difficult and often treacherous conditions. A *Western Morning News* special correspondent referred to Berlin as a 'dead city'. Some, trying to make light of a bleak December in the torn city, were more allegorical, singing 'Dreaming of a Red Christmas'. Crooner Bing Crosby would have been none too happy.

Ten days before Christmas the inevitable happened: a British soldier was shot and seriously wounded by a member of a Red Army patrol. In what were clearly the actions of an over-zealous trooper, the Russian fired into Private Charles Knill's back with a submachine gun, described as having been at 'very close range'. A further six British soldiers were apprehended and led away by the Russian patrol. Soviet General Laurentiv and Colonel J. Meadmore of the British commander-in-chief's mission to the Soviet occupation forces, met at the scene to investigate the incident. Tension in the area was palpable.

In a reconstruction of events based on statements from the British soldiers, it transpired that the Tommies had been on a rabbit hunt when one of their party inadvertently and unknowingly crossed the ill-defined Soviet-zone boundary while tracking a wounded animal. His comrades watched him run into a copse of trees before hearing the crack of a weapon being discharged. Moments later they watched with shock and horror as armed Russian soldiers marched the hapless Knill away, his arms extended above his head in a gesture of surrender. A British captain, accompanied by three unarmed NCOs and five privates, headed to the boundary at Duderstadt to plead for Knill's release.

RECORD £1,500,000 POPPY DAY TARGET

Long before dawn today, the first poppy sellers were out in the streets of England and Wales with their trays of emblems and collecting boxes for Remembrance Day. This year the target set by the British Legion was £1,500,000, although the greatest amount ever collected on a Remembrance Day so far was £1,000,000 in 1945.

For the first time, official consent was received from the Ministry of Civil Aviation for poppies to be sold at British airports, and wherever a British air service touched down throughout the world, the Flanders Poppy was for sale.

Seven thousand poppies were sent for British troop in Berlin, 3,000 on the airlift and 4,000 by RAF transport.

Tonight the King will buy his poppy from Lady Brunel Cohen, before leaving Buckingham Palace for the Remembrance Day festival at the Royal Albert Hall. The Queen is still confined indoors, recovering from an influenza cold.

Gloucester Citizen, Saturday, 6 November 1948

All they encountered was the incoherent ranting of a Soviet sentry, gesticulating wildly with his rifle in the air. The guard fired a shot, ostensibly to attract the attention of his superior, but by discharging his weapon, he instead alerted a sizeable group of Russian troops who advanced from a farmhouse 200 yards distant towards the unsuspecting British men. Their captors added to their comrade's shouting and, surrounding the Tommies, started firing into the air. Their undisciplined fervour, fuelled by their success in catching the enemy 'red-handed', could only have a catastrophic outcome. A burst of small-arms fire struck Knill in the back, causing him to drop to the ground.

The six soldiers of the Oxfordshire and Buckinghamshire Light Infantry, who were taken prisoner by the Russians, were released four days later. Private Knill, 19 years old and a native of Cornwall, was recovering in a German civil hospital where, after two blood transfusions, 'good hopes were entertained for his recovery'.

On the eve of Christmas, in a move interpreted by Moscow as a prelude to the remilitarization of Berlin, Britain, France and the United States established a unitary three-power military administration. The tripartite agreement was part of a rationalisation of the Allies' presence in occupied Berlin, based on the assertion that the Russians' refusal to attend Four-Power meetings since walking out six months ago, 'cannot be allowed any longer to obstruct proper administration of Berlin'. The door would be left open should they wish to resume their position on the four-nation council.

On the last day of 1948, airlift aircraft made the 100,000th flight of the relief programme into Berlin, having carried a total of 700,000 tons. For the staff of the mammoth undertaking, however, it was just another tiring day in ice and snow, punctuated by now routine daily protests to the Soviet military authorities about 'exercises' in and near the air corridors, including the intimidation of Allied aircraft by Russian Yak fighters.

Major General E. O. Herbert, British commandant in Berlin, declared in a New Year message, 'The airlift is rising and the shortest day is over. The people of Berlin will win through.'

6. SMALL MOVEMENTS OF THE BOA CONSTRICTOR

In Allied messes throughout West Berlin, the less than sanguine strains of 'Auld Lang Syne' sounded the knell of a dismal 1948 for the city's long-suffering German population. It appeared to the *Volk* of Hitler's *Vaterland* that the collective punishing burden of debt owed for their Fuhrer's crimes against humanity would be visited on them for generations to come.

Early in the new year, the British administration in Berlin addressed the lassitude that permeated the very soul of the city's embattled citizenry. In an 85-page booklet bearing the unassuming title *Notes on the Blockade of Berlin, 1948*, they assured their German wards that the British community 'is very much alive, busy, and on the job'. Blame for the 'present difficulties' was laid squarely at the feet of the Russians:

> The measures which constitute the blockade were by no means introduced all at one moment nor, for that matter, may they yet be complete.
>
> With oriental deviousness and intricacy, the pattern was gradually displayed.
>
> There was accumulative series of innumerable moves, like the small movements of the boa constrictor, each of them barely noticeable and difficult to describe, but none the less important.

RUSSIA SENDING BACK SHIPS WE LENT

The homecoming of British warships, including the battleship *Royal Sovereign*, which we lent to Russia in 1944, begins on January 15.

The *Royal Sovereign*, which the Russians renamed *Archangelsk*, leaves Murmansk for Rosyth [Royal Navy base on the east coast of Scotland] on that date, together with a destroyer and three submarines she had on loan, the Admiralty announced last night.

The ships – 12 in number – are being returned under the agreement, as Russia is now receiving her share of the Italian fleet.

The eight destroyers are: *St Albans, Brighton, Richmond, Chelsea, Leamington, Roxburgh, Georgetown,* and *Lincoln.* ['Town' class]

The three submarines are: *Unbroken, Unison,* and *Ursula.* [Undine or 'U' Class]

The ships, manned by personnel of the Soviet Navy, will arrive in three groups. The second group is expected to arrive in March and the third in July.

The Flag Officer, Scotland and Northern Ireland [Admiral Sir Ernest Russell Archer] is in charge of the transfer arrangements at Rosyth.

Western Morning News, Friday, 7 January 1949

Above left: British military police erecting sector-boundary signage.

Above right: Soviet air ace, Captain Mayorov in the cockpit of his Lavochkin La-5.

Since then a whole series of measures have gradually been drawing the net tighter. Short of physically closing every street between the sectors and deploying still more troops and police, the blockade is almost as tight as it can be made.

The blockade is, however, psychological rather than economic. In the Soviet sector the Russians offer blandishments of every sort – more food, sweets for the children, more coal, more consumer goods – if the people of the Western sectors will sign themselves over to Russian domination.

It matters little that the people of the Soviet zone (as distinct from sector) cannot be given the same things. The eye absorbs more than the ear, or so they hope.

Meanwhile, British analysts tallied airlift statistics up to the end of 1948. In this six-month period an incomprehensible 13,000,000 miles were flown by Royal Air Force aircraft globally, in which 175,000 tons were carried. In total, Royal Air Force crews had amassed a staggering 900,000 flying hours, of which 416,000 hours alone were attributed to home commands, including the British Air Forces of Occupation (BAFO), i.e. the Berlin airlift. The second highest number of hours logged came from Flying Training Command, including the Rhodesian Air Training Group (RATG), running up 263,100 hours. This was a direct reflection of the added manpower pressures that the airlift was having on the RAF.

The magnitude of Soviet threats to the safety of the airlift in the same time frame was far less known – perhaps blissfully so. British and American chief controllers at the Berlin air-safety centre, in lodging yet another routine protest against Soviet air-firing exercises in the Fassberg air corridor, prompted a spokesman to report that the number of protests now runs into 'well over three figures'.

On 18 January the three Western occupation authorities, in the first positive move to play the Russians at their own game, imposed a counter-blockade of the Soviet sector of Berlin. The embargo, in retaliation for the Soviet blocking of the shipment of goods to the three Western sectors, directed that no consignments of products from the West would be allowed to enter the Russian sector without an Allied permit. In a move seen by critics as long overdue, a total ban was simultaneously placed on scarce items such as radio transmitters, steel alloys, dies and cutting tools. Less essential items may be exported to the Russians at the 'discretion' of the Allies.

Since the introduction of relief aid to the city of Berlin, the British military authorities had placed particular emphasis on the provision of health and welfare assistance to the city's vulnerable. It was therefore not uncommon to find return flights ferrying orphaned or undernourished children, and those in need of critical medical attention to the Allied sectors. In such irregular circumstances, however, such civilians had to face the same risks as those endured by overtired aircrews operating in hazardous winter conditions.

On the night of 24 January, a C-47 Dakota, en route to the British zone with 25 people on board, crashed in dense fog inside the Soviet zone. Of the 22 civilian passengers, 17 were malnourished German children being taken to new homes in the British zone. There were eight fatalities, including a member of the RAF crew. The German police station at nearby Schoenberg reported 17 injuries – two of them serious – including three children and two of the three-man flight crew. The Soviet authorities said they had sent emergency medical aid, while at the same time an RAF crash party from Lübeck crossed into the Soviet zone to render assistance.

Berlin's children were amongst the most vulnerable during the blockade. Private Wynne Evans from Wales has a reassuring chat.

The mercy flight took off from Gatow at 5.00 pm that evening, its route to Lübeck almost entirely over Soviet territory. At 9.30 pm, the RAF airfield at Lübeck reported the flight as two and a half hours overdue. Just after midnight, after responding to a report by a local farmer that he had seen an aircraft in trouble with its landing lights on, the Russians reported to the British that they had located the wreckage. On impact with the ground, the aircraft had burst into flames. It was reported that the Russians had rushed every available rescue and medical unit to the crash site, where a makeshift dressing station was set up. RAF officers said that, at the time of the crash, the cloud ceiling was at 600 feet, with heavy mist and drizzle. Visibility was a mile. Fog brought the airlift to a total halt as all three Allied terminals in Berlin suffered from dangerously low levels of visibility.

The Soviet-licensed Berliner *Zeitung* immediately accused the British evacuation by air of undernourished German children as 'political murder', adding that the children who perished in the Dakota disaster would still be alive had the Western allies not blockaded Berlin.

Then suddenly, on 30 January, the hitherto taciturn Soviet leader and dictator Joseph Stalin broke his long silence, saying that he was ready to append his name to a joint declaration that neither the Soviet Union nor the United States had any intention of taking up arms against the other. He added that he had 'no objections to meeting US President Truman at a mutually agreeable venue to discuss the mechanisms to conclude such a peace treaty'. 'Suitable' meeting places in Russia, Poland or Czechoslovakia were included, on the premise that Stalin had received medical advice against long-distance travel by sea or air.

For someone well known for saying that he didn't trust anyone including himself, Stalin's ostensible softening of heart lacked credibility, let alone honesty. Was this just another Moscow ploy to play for time so that they could start their own nuclear arsenal? He offered to cooperate with the Americans in gradual bilateral disarmament measures, saying he would lift his blockade of Berlin if the United States, Britain and France lifted theirs, and agreed to suspend their plans to establish a separate West German government.

Stalin's 'red bait' was also construed as an attempt at distracting the Allies from forming their own North Atlantic defence alliance. At the same time, Russia's Scandinavian neighbours failed to reach consensus on any form of defensive pact free of alliances, as explained by Norwegian premier Einar Gerhardsen when he said that each of the three countries assessed their security issues and needs differently. In a note described by Norwegian Foreign Minister Halvard Lange as 'factual, calm and polite', Moscow deemed it opportune to remind Oslo that they shared a common border with the Soviet Union. A diplomatic correspondent in London interpreted the Soviet missive for what it was: a very thinly veiled threat, and an attempt by the Russians to influence the manner in which Norway conducted her foreign policies.

Stalin was not desirous of a mass mobilisation of American and European forces in Europe, but as a Western commentator put it, the West was wary of 'thorns in Stalin's olive branch'.

In equally sceptical tones, in Paris the Popular Republican Party organ *L'Aube* accused Moscow of attempting to sabotage peace. In a reference to British prime minister Neville Chamberlain's naïve 'peace for our time' speech in 1938 after a visit with Adolf Hitler in Munich, the paper added that Stalin was 'inviting Truman to come to Munich'.

Needless to say, Truman's response was one of rejection: no to a non-aggression pact, no to a meeting anywhere behind the Iron Curtain, and no to bilateral talks – other interested parties would have to be invited to the table. Washington stated that they would consider

The massive damage inflicted by Allied ten-ton bombs on German towns and cities, such as Hamm.

RUSSIA BACKS ISRAEL AGAINST BRITAIN

It was officially announced in Tel Aviv yesterday that Israel had made a 'strong protest' to the United Nations representative in Palestine against the landing of British troops at Transjordan's Red Sea port of Akaba, near the Palestinian frontier, and a demand the UNO observers should be sent to prevent British violation of the Israeli frontier.

The Russian minister to Israel, Pavel Yershoff, yesterday called on Mr Moshe Shertok, Israeli foreign minister, and according to political sources in Tel Aviv, offered Israel Soviet support in view of the 'deteriorating situation'. Mr Shertok was said to have replied that the Israeli government did not feel the situation was grave enough, but promised to keep the Soviet minister informed.

Dr Ralph Bunche, Acting Palestinian Mediator, said in New York last night that he had asked United Nations observers to make the 'fullest possible check' on both sides of the Egypt-Palestine frontier into the shooting down of an RAF aircraft [by Israeli forces].

[The independent Jewish state of Israel was declared on 14 May 1948, but only recognised a full year later]

Northern Whig, Monday, 10 January 1949

'any proposals consistent with their commitments and obligations', and would discuss Germany and any other issues as soon as the Berlin question was resolved and the Russian blockade lifted – *not* before. Stalin was also reminded that both their countries, and other member-states of the UN, were already 'pledged by the most solemn treaty commitments in the United Nations Charter not to engage in war against each other'.

American Secretary of State, Dean Acheson, in his detailed, point-by-point reply to Stalin, clearly spelled out America's unbending stance: 'The interest of the United States and all of the hundreds of millions of people in the world in peace is so fundamental that the matter of peace cannot be tampered with as an instrument in any international political manoeuvre. It will not be used by the United States.'

Acheson pointed out that his country had led the way in disarmament, but claimed that Soviet delegates obstructed the efforts of participating nations to implement those clauses of the UN charter designed for the peaceful resolution of disputes. It was also the Soviet delegation to the United Nations General Assembly that refused to play a part in any arrangements to introduce the effective international regulation of atomic energy. The question of a West German government was not open for debate: 'The preparatory work ... was going forward as necessary for accomplishment of the responsibilities of the three Western Powers.'

Truman, in calculated timing, then added muscle to his rebuff of the Soviet leader. At midnight on 5 February, the flow of *all* goods traffic from the British and American sectors to the Soviet sector was suspended. Other Western Europe nations were informed of the Anglo-American move, as the embargo also applied to goods ostensibly in transit through their sectors into the Soviet zone. A statement from the British military government made it clear that, 'Although the Soviet authorities had a long start with their blockade measures, they must know that they are getting the worst of the exchange.'

The much-vaunted Soviet zone two-year economic plan would not be sustainable without the much-needed inflow of the necessary raw materials, machinery and equipment, all of which the British and American administrations in Berlin had now cut off. Pig-iron output and the production of basic chemicals had fallen to as low as 60 percent of the 1948 targets. The textile industries in Saxony in the Soviet zone were only operating at half capacity, while the railway reconstruction budget for the current fiscal year was cut by 75 percent.

'No better progress has been made than in the supply of food. We have now raised the standard of living to which the German people have enough to eat.' In mid-February, American military governor General Lucius Clay published a report declaring that the situation in Germany 'paints a pretty good picture'. Elaborating on his assessment of the German nation since the demise of the Third Reich, he confidently suggested that history would prove the military administrations right by entrusting the German people themselves with the 'denazification' process of their own fractured nation.

Meaningful progress had been made towards the establishment of independent media, singling out the French dynamiting in December of the transmitter towers of the Soviet-controlled Berlin radio as a 'tremendous uplift' to morale in the Western sector. The capital's morale received a further boost that month when the city's election results revealed that a massive 86 percent of the eligible electorate backed the anti-communist parties.

Meanwhile, the progress of time brought with it an inordinate amount of experience in air logistics for Berlin's military governments.

Above left: An atomic bomb test at the Bikini Atoll test site on 1 July 46.

Above right: British and Russian military police patrol Berlin streets at night, a routine that was introduced on 30 December 1945.

Early in 1949, measures to improve airlift efficiency were introduced, including a rearrangement of aircraft routing into Berlin, and the introduction of an innovative new unloading procedure at RAF Gatow. To rationalise the distribution of airfreight across the Berlin airfields, aircraft operating from Fassberg, Fuhlsbuttel and Schleswigland – American Skymasters, civil cargo aircraft, RAF Hastings and some of the civil tankers – commenced operating into Tegel, the recently completed runway in the French sector. Aircraft from Celle, Wunstorf and Lübeck – Skymasters, RAF and civil Yorks, civil tankers and RAF Dakotas – were all redirected into Gatow.

Improved unloading systems, developed in conjunction with army teams on the ground, involved the use of a jeep that was in two-way radio contact with a special control tower dedicated solely to the airlift-unloading operation. The flow of all traffic in and out of the unloading bays was coordinated from the tower, using the jeep driver to implement and troubleshoot on the ground. As the unloading process neared completion, aircrews in the lounge were alerted to get ready for their next sortie.

On 18 February, the one millionth ton of the Anglo-American relief airlift arrived at RAF Gatow. Flying from the Wunstorf airport in the British zone, an RAF York carried 7½ tons of meat, flour, potatoes, butter and hay. As the aircraft taxied towards the unloading concourse, it was flying a blue pennant inscribed with '1,000,000 tons'. Commanded by New Zealander Squadron Leader Eric Best, with the officer commanding British Air Forces of Occupation,

RUSSIA KNEW JAPAN'S WAR PLANS

The United States Army today disclosed the story of a pre-war Russian spy ring which robbed the Japanese cabinet and the German embassy in Tokyo of secrets that helped to turn the tide of war.

A 40,000-word report by General Headquarters, Far Eastern Command issued in Washington, told how for nine years a daring and skilful band of spies worked for Soviet Russia in Japan, under a German, Dr Richard Sorge.

From 1932 until its uncovering, shortly before Pearl Harbour, the ring looted the Japanese cabinet and the German embassy in Tokyo of top-secret information. It went unsuspected until October 1941.

Sorge was able to keep the Soviet fully informed on Japanese military and industrial potential. The Red Army always knew current Japanese plans, and could make its own plans and dispositions accordingly, the report said.

Sorge himself lived on trusted terms with the German ambassador in Tokyo and his staff. Sorge's chief lieutenant, a Japanese named Ozaki Hozumi, was on equally close terms with Prince Konoe, then prime minister.

Both the chief spies ended their careers on the gallows, but for many years they obtained masses of information on every useful subject, transmitting their intelligence to Soviet Russia by concealed radio, by courier and through the Soviet embassy.

As German armies smashed into Western Russia and great Soviet military installations there were destroyed, Sorge and his companions were able to assure Russia that the Japanese would not attack, and Siberian divisions were then sent for the successful defence of Moscow.

Although most of the principals are dead, some are still alive, the report remarked. 'They can be expected to be busy at their trade at this very moment in the capitals of the world.'

Hull Daily Mail, Thursday, 10 February 1949

Berlin's burghers were often required to work for food.

Air Marshal Thomas Melling his co-pilot, the first attempt at landing had to be aborted due to the 'worst fog of the winter'. A second radar-assisted landing was successful. Fog grounded the whole airlift for an unbroken 42 hours.

A week later, daily airlift tonnages exceeded 7,500 for the first time.

In a move that fuelled considerable speculation and some shock, Radio Moscow announced on 4 March that Soviet Foreign Minister Molotov had been replaced. The Presidium of the Supreme Soviet replaced the 59-year-old Molotov with Andrei Vyshinsky. Born in Poland of 'rich bourgeois parents', the 66-year-old Vyshinsky, a member of the Soviet delegation to the Potsdam Conference in 1945, led his nation's delegation to the first General Assembly of the United Nations in London in 1946. Trained in legal matters, Vyshinsky was renowned for his acerbic attacks on the Western powers. General opinion in the West believed that Molotov was either being promoted to continue serving as Stalin's right-hand man, or was to take charge of the emerging superpower's economic rehabilitation and the maintenance of Soviet armed might. There was also a strong train of thought that Molotov was being groomed as a successor to Stalin.

Two days later, 'Berlin reports' stated that Stalin and Molotov, their relationship already strained for some time, had almost come to blows in the Kremlin. There could only be one loser in such an untenable situation, if indeed this was the case.

By early spring 1949, few could doubt that the Allied airlift into Berlin was a monumental success. The city's burghers had adapted well to a regime of Spartan proportions, while the airlift operation had become a well-oiled routine. Moscow's stranglehold on the capital was weakening.

With most bridges in Germany destroyed, Allied Bailey bridges were extensively used, remaining in place for many years after the end of the war.

Moscow's Red Square in the 1940s.

In a morale-boosting coup, the airlift brought a spring fashion show to the glamour-starved *fraus* and *frauleins* of Berlin. Hundreds of women queued for hours to catch a glimpse of the latest in Western fashion, shown off on the catwalk by models given appropriately relevant sobriquets: Blocade, Air Bridge, East and West. The immensely successful event featured 'low necks, three-quarter-length sleeves, wide billowy skirts and bare-backed evening dresses'.

The general public were also tiring of the Berlin impasse. Consequently, the collapse of another 'well-meant' attempt at reaching an agreement yet again passed by virtually unnoticed. Addressing the currency issue – the principal cause of the Soviet blockade – in the UN Security Council, neutral members failed to agree on the adoption of a basis for further discussion. Whilst the vision of a single currency for Germany remained remotely improbable, the airlift continued without relent in its tenth month of operations. Talk in global political corridors more and more believed that the dispute had run for so long that a settlement of the currency issue no longer guaranteed a lifting of the blockade. The Soviet military government in Berlin had forced a finite division of Berlin's civil administration, thereby making the universal scenario substantially more complex.

No progress could be made in 'a fog of doubt and suspicion'.

On Sunday, 20 March, the American, British and French military governors issued a joint declaration stating that the Soviet-sector marks would cease to be legal tender in Berlin's three Western sectors. Under new regulations that came into effect the following day, the so-called Western mark would be the sole legal currency in the Allied sectors. With an imbalance in

Major Stevens, the British military government officer responsible for education, in a Berlin classroom.

value of five to one, the disparity meant that city workers paid in the much weaker Eastern mark were at an immediate disadvantage when it came to spending their pay packet. Work skills became secondary in importance to the currency in which you were paid. There had been no currency review or reform since the Soviets imposed the blockade on the city, but the Allied authorities stressed that their decision had been a financial and not a political counter-measure against the Soviet sector.

It was, however, not lost on Moscow that the unilateral currency reform was introduced at the same time as the publication of the terms of the new Atlantic Treaty. Inherent in the proposed defence pact was the assimilation of both West Berlin and West Germany into the new transnational security regime. This, in turn, conveyed a very clear message to the world that the Western powers were there to stay.

American military governor Brigadier General Frank Howley used the West's currency move to call on the Soviet Union to lift its failed blockade of Berlin. Encouraging their erstwhile allies to 'shake the hand which we've never refused to give them', Howley said, 'It must be obvious, even to the most dense Communist, that their tactics have failed. Neither the Soviet blockade at the Elbe nor the ice of winter stopped the airlift. It must be obvious that it would be to their own selfish interests to discontinue these tactics which have caused more trouble to them than to us.'

On 4 April 1949, a collective peace pact was signed in Washington, primarily to balance Moscow's military might on Western Europe's doorstep. The member states included the five signatories to the 1948 Brussels Treaty – Britain, France, Belgium, the Netherlands and Luxembourg – together with the United States, Canada, Portugal, Italy, Norway, Denmark and Iceland – the latter reluctantly so. The first NATO secretary general, the Right Honourable the Lord Hastings 'Pug' Ismay, succinctly declared that the organisation's goal was 'to keep the Russians out, the Americans in, and the Germans down'.

JEWS RIOT AT CINEMA

Following renewed rioting by Jews in Berlin this afternoon, in which a British officer was beaten up and police used clubs and fire hoses to stop charging demonstrators, Mr Henry Durban, Berlin representative of the J. Arthur Rank Organisation, has decided not to continue showing the British film 'Oliver Twist'. Crowds stormed the theatre yesterday when the film was first shown.

Jews, who received reinforcements, today repeatedly attacked the German police with stones and succeeded in breaking through a cordon. Smashing doors of the cinema, they gained entry and the performance was stopped. British military police, called to the scene, refused to interfere.

When news that the film would be withdrawn became known, demonstrators sang the Israeli National Anthem.

Yorkshire Evening Post, Monday, 21 February 1949

The Soviets in Eastern Germany, anticipating the event in Washington, launched a caustic anti-West propaganda campaign under a typically Red Flag slogan: 'Down with the Atlantic Pact ... the conspiracy against world peace.' With the day of the 'downtrodden international worker' only weeks away, the German Communists ordered that this message be 'drummed unceasingly to the German people'.

In Washington, that champion of anti-Communist sentiment, President Truman, ignored the Soviet rhetoric, electing instead to respond with a material gesture towards his new European allies. Following the NATO signing ceremony, several hundred American aircraft would be taken out of storage and transferred to Europe to bolster the air defences of member states; Britain alone asked for up to 200 Boeing B-29 Superfortresses. In addition to land-based aircraft, America would also supply surplus artillery and machine guns.

Soviet troops and tanks muster in front of the devastated Brandenburg Gate.

Truman now also took a page out of Stalin's book of strutting one's military prowess. United States Army Day was commemorated in occupied Germany on 6 April, with an uninhibited programme of ceremonies, reviews and parades. American commander in Europe and American military governor General Lucius Clay was reviewing officer at a massed parade of American forces at Grafenwöhr in Bavaria. Berlin hosted three separate parades, while American jet fighters circled over Nuremberg.

Addressing nearly 5,000 crack American troops, Clay said, 'You are a symbol of our country's firm will to fight for the rights of free men. We have joined the Atlantic community and pledged ourselves to secure peace and prevent aggression by force if necessary.' He added that the shipping lanes used by the American Navy to ferry supplies to the Berlin airlift would be kept clear, even if that meant using 'fighting navy craft'. Hundreds of tanks, guns and armoured vehicles paraded past the saluting dais, which was bedecked with American, British and French flags.

In Washington, the State Department announced that America would officially ignore protests from the Soviet Union against the formation of NATO. Meanwhile, British Foreign Secretary Bevin's extended visit to Washington, where he was holding prolonged meetings with his French and American counterparts, fuelled fresh speculation in diplomatic and political circles that a lifting of the Berlin blockade may be close. It also did not pass unnoticed that, for the first time, the Soviet authorities in Germany partially relaxed their ban on the Western deutschmark by permitting stations in West Berlin to accept the currency in payment for electric-railway fares.

Days later, the foreign ministers meeting in Washington finally went public on what Bevin referred to as a 'momentous week'. At a brief conference and signing ceremony, American Secretary of State Acheson, French Foreign Minister Schuman and Bevin issued a joint communiqué about a new occupation policy that 'aims to permit the German people to exercise self-government'. The tripartite agreement redefined Allied responsibility and control of occupied Germany, identifying the 'machinery' needed to return the disarmed nation to the Western European fold. A buoyant Bevin spoke of a policy of 'negative control' of a nation that had twice brought the world into global bloodshed of Biblical proportions, while gradually apportioning greater autonomy with time.

The Atlantic pact, and now the Washington agreement, placed the Western allies in a much stronger bargaining position with Moscow. The Russians' persistent refusal to sit around a table with the Allies to reach an amicable solution to the Berlin crisis had in itself nurtured a closing of the ranks to the west of the Iron Curtain. Shielded by the atomic might of America, Europe and NATO would now determine Germany's future.

On 14 April, the Soviet Union took their displeasure of the formation of NATO to the United Nations. Moscow's permanent representative to the UN, Andrei 'Mr Nyet' Gromyko, in a scathing attack on the West, described the Atlantic pact as 'a weapon of aggression aimed against the Soviet Union'. In a 6,000-word address, Gromyko spoke of the West's master plan 'to dictate, to isolate Russia, and to unleash a new war'. He accused the British and Americans of breaking the tripartite policy agreements of Teheran, Potsdam and Yalta, and of being in breach of the Anglo-Soviet Treaty of 1942 – a 20-year, post-war military and political alliance signed in London by the then British foreign secretary Anthony Eden and Soviet foreign minister Vyacheslav Molotov. Rejecting a proposed resolution curtailing veto parameters in the Security Council, Gromyko asserted that 'the use of the atom bomb was part of the United States war aims'.

Above: Another
American atomic test at
Bikini Atoll, in 1946.

Left: Bomb craters
straddle a bridge
over the Rhine.
Rebuilding the German
transport infrastructure
would take many years
at enormous expense,
largely met from the
spoils of war.

In a formal response to Moscow, the Foreign Office's missive to the Soviet Embassy in London was resolute and unapologetic in its message:

The foreign ministers of the countries assembled here in Washington for the signing of the North Atlantic Pact ... note that the views expressed by the Soviet Government on the 31st March, are identical in their misrepresentation of the nature and intent of this association with those published by the Soviet Foreign Office in January, before the text of the Pact was even in existence. It would appear thus that the views of the Soviet Government on this subject do not arise from an examination of the character and text of the North Atlantic Pact, but from other considerations.

The text of the treaty itself is the best answer to such misrepresentations and allegations. The text makes clear the completely defensive nature of this Pact, its conformity with both the spirit and letter of the Charter of the United Nations, and also the fact that the Pact is not directed against any nation or group of nations, but only against armed aggression.

His Majesty's Government cannot admit that the North Atlantic Treaty is contrary to Article 7 of the British-Soviet Treaty of 1942, since, as shown above, the North Atlantic Treaty is directed solely against aggression itself.

For their part [His Majesty's Government], they have done their utmost to cooperate with the Soviet Union and with other Allied and friendly governments and, in the words of Article 5 of the British-Soviet Treaty, 'to work together in close and friendly collaboration after the re-establishment of peace for the organisation of security and economic prosperity in Europe'.

In the Soviet zone of Germany, the Soviet authorities have violated every relevant clause of the Potsdam agreement, and their actions culminated in the blockade of Berlin. His Majesty's Government also fail to understand how the Soviet Government interpret their obligation under Article 5 of the British-Soviet Treaty, 'not to seek territorial aggrandisement for themselves and not to interfere in the internal affairs of other states'.

The Western world is now consolidating its economic and political recovery, and its people can fortunately look forward to a brighter future. There is no reason why the Soviet Government should regard the return of strength and prosperity to the West as aggressive or contrary to their interests.

The Scotsman, Thursday, 14 April 1949

In Berlin, American military government commander General Clay announced an increase in the size of America's airlift fleet, while in Washington, Congress approved a £1.3 billion Marshall Aid to Europe tranche for the next 15 months. In the 24-hour period up to midday Saturday, 16 April, the combined Anglo-American airlift transported a massive 11,600 metric tons, totally smashing the previous record of 7,467 tons. Traffic control reported, in ideal flying conditions, that airlift aircraft were landing at the air terminals of Gatow, Tempelhof and Tegel at a rate of one every two minutes.

The tireless Clay told a Reuters correspondent, 'As far as I am concerned, the situation remains absolutely unchanged, and the airlift will go on as long as it is needed. I find no grounds for optimism at all. I think that our counter-blockade is putting pressure on the Soviet zone, but I do not think that this is decisive.'

Towards the end of April, rumours about an imminent lifting of the Soviet blockade were so widespread that the London stock market reacted bullishly. In an attempt seen by many as diplomatic posturing to deflect attention away from the real issue, the official Soviet news agency,

---

RAF TO AID CHINA BRITONS?

An emergency airlift evacuation for the British community in Shanghai is being arranged by the RAF, it was reported today.

Aircraft were said to be waiting at Hong Kong and Singapore ready to take off for Shanghai. It was estimated that it would take two days to move out the British community if the necessity arose.

Meanwhile, garrison headquarters today announced that 4,000 Communist troops had begun to push eastwards from Soochow along the Nanking-Shanghai railway. Skirmishes were being fought near Weiting, about 10 miles east of Soochow.

It was officially confirmed in Hong Kong that the RAF had been ordered to stand by to take part in a Shanghai airlift.

Lincolnshire Echo, Thursday, 28 April 1949

Tass, stated that Western press reports of a possible lifting of the blockade 'did not correspond with reality'. Arriving in London in the early hours of 26 April, the statement said that the US ambassador-at-large Philip Jessup had approached his Soviet counterpart, Yakov Malik, as long ago as 15 February. This had been in response to Stalin seeking clarification from a Western correspondent about what he was alleged to have said about the Berlin blockade and a single currency. Tass said that it refuted 'incorrect rumours' primarily fuelled by 'the American press'.

Tass made it clear that Moscow would agree to simultaneous lifting of the blockade and 'traffic restrictions' provided that a firm date is set for a meeting of the full Council of Foreign Ministers. This would also no longer depend on a long-standing proviso that a uniform currency be introduced in Berlin. This had all been conveyed to Dr Jessup by Malik on 21 March.

The state of play had now been revealed for all to see. As the diplomatic tempo quickened, representatives from Britain, France and the United States had met and reached 'an agreed position'. On 26 April, Dr Jessup finalised his preparations for a meeting with Malik by calling at the White House to discuss blockade-lifting proposals with President Truman. The following day, Jessup and Malik met at the Soviet delegation headquarters in New York, giving cause for guarded optimism that the Four-Power Council of Foreign Ministers would reconvene soon. Talk was now of the blockade being lifted 'within 30 days'.

The Americans asked Moscow for a specific timetable giving precise details as to when and on what conditions they would lift the blockade. In a note delivered by Jessup to Malik at the United Nations, a written formalisation of determining procedures was requested.

On the ground, arrangements were made to resume passenger and goods rail traffic as soon as the blockade was lifted. In Hanover, the first passenger bus made an uninterrupted journey from Berlin to Hanover. In a seemingly mundane event, a glimmer of hope for the Soviets' sincerity this time round, the bus passengers said they were 'very politely received' by the Russian staff manning the control point.

The American air force meanwhile lifted the veil of secrecy from the 'secret weapon' that was behind the recent substantial increases in tonnages flown by their airlift aircraft. The partially declassified new radar apparatus, CPS-5, enabled traffic controllers to detect incoming aircraft

German POWs, such as these at Normandy, did not have long to wait to be repatriated to a post-war Germany. Hundreds of thousands taken prison by the Red Army, however, were not so fortunate, disappearing into the Soviet Gulag forever.

when they were still 50 to 70 miles out. The operators would then regulate the pilot's direction, speed and altitude to their designated airport, ensuring that correct approach intervals were maintained for optimum efficiency. Once pilots reached final approach, ground operators at the respective destinations would guide them in. On Easter Saturday, 1,400 sorties carted just over 12,000 tons of supplies into Berlin.

Even at this delicate eleventh hour, however, and while the world was watching Moscow, the Soviet military authorities could not desist from their almost-routine acts of disruption and flexing of muscle.

On 28 April, submachine-gun-toting Soviet troops arrogantly crossed into the British and French sectors where they occupied three canal locks, preventing barges with airlift supplies from proceeding. In a no-nonsense display of zero-tolerance, Major J. Hughes of the Gordon Highlanders deployed British military police in armoured cars to 'retake' Charlottenburg Lock in the British zone. Additional British troops secured the other two locks, maintaining an all-night guard. A British spokesman said that they could not tolerate any interference with canal traffic.

Not since the August 1948 Potsdamer Platz riots had armed military units from East and West confronted each other in like manner. The Soviet troops at the locks, described as being 'ill at ease', informed the British interpreter that they were acting under orders. Surprised by their not disagreeable attitude, and 'astonished at their politeness', British officers were informed by the Russians that they would spend the night at the locks, so that in the morning they would again block the canal barges.

Transport officer for the British Control Commission, George Fletcher, said of the uncomfortable situation, 'We have enough troops here and standing by to cover anything. We have been instructed to avoid bloodshed and avoid trouble.'

In a further act of provocation, this time in the Brandenburg province, Soviet Yak fighters conducted air-to-ground firing 'exercises' in a Berlin airlift corridor. Showing total disregard for the verbal protest from the British, American and French military governments, the firing continued for a further 11 hours.

All British troops would be confined to barracks on May Day, 1 May, in anticipation of massed anti-Communist and anti-Western demonstrations.

Left: A Red Army sniper with a Mosin-Nagant Model 1930 bolt-action rifle. Designed by Russian Sergei Mosin, it had a five-round internal box magazine.

Below: The blown-up Palace Bridge over the River Spree in Berlin. The restoration of the capital's infrastructure would take many years and at great expense.

On the morning of Thursday, 5 November, the United Kingdom and Europe woke up to the news that months of rumour and speculation had finally given way to fact: the Berlin blockade would be lifted on 12 May.

In a communiqué issued by the French foreign office, the participant Four-Power nations declared that all restrictions on traffic, including those of the Allies' counter-embargo, would be scrapped. This will be followed on 23 May by a meeting in Paris of the Council of Foreign Ministers.

In Berlin, the anticipation escalated as a British transport official announced that the trains were ready to run to Berlin, stating that 'the whole railway handling organisation has been kept on its toes during the ten months of blockade.'

America, however, viewed the dramatic Soviet turnaround with a great deal of qualified scepticism, and, indeed, suspicion. The diplomatic correspondent for the *New York Times*, in a leading article, summed up the American mood:

United States officials had faith in the Marshall Plan, airlift, West German Republic, and North Atlantic Treaty policy. But the lifting of the blockade introduces a large element of doubt into their lives ... it was only too evident that the end of the Berlin blockade does not mean the end of the Cold War, and the events in China [civil war] raise in some minds, at least, the question of who, on balance, is winning it. But there can be no question of the Western success in Berlin, as in all Western Europe. If there is one compensation for the dangers and sacrifices involved, it is that in Berlin the Soviets met their first and, for Europe, possibly decisive defeat.

MIRACLE OF THE AIRLIFT

Captain Michael Bowen, 44th Royal Tank Regiment and member of the Western Daily Press and Bristol Mirror staff, just back from Berlin comments:

'It was on June 28 last year that the airlift began. Entry into Berlin by road, rail and canal was suddenly prohibited, and the capital, marooned nearly 100 miles in the Soviet sector, could only be reached by air. It seemed incredible that sufficient supplies to keep the Western Berliners fed and warm could be sent in by air. But soon that was exactly what did happen, and as the organisation improved, life in Berlin became less and less austere.

It was of course a fabulously uneconomic method of transport. The ration of goods carried to petrol consumed must have been very small. Wastage was enormous. The sacks which carried coal into Berlin for example, lasted only one or two journeys.

It was all worked out so carefully, that one aircraft would land, another take off, and a third land, all on the same runway, within three minutes.

The Army was involved in the airlift as well. As soon as the propellers stopped, the Army came into the picture, being responsible for moving, checking and storing the supplies. RASC [Royal Army Service Corps] officers superintended the hard-working Germans. Flying supplies into Berlin was made easier by the German habit of building their airfields near a railway, and the distance from railhead to aircraft was often only a few hundred yards.

Western Daily Press, Thursday, 5 May 1949

It therefore came as little surprise when American Air Force officials announced that 'the Berlin airlift machine – its planes, men and directors – probably will be kept in a standby condition in Europe until it is reasonably certain Russia is not planning another blockade'.

At 5.35 am on Thursday, 12 May, the first train, carrying British and American personnel, arrived at Charlottenburg station. The train was piped across the border by Gordon Highlanders, who had been travelling on the historic train – appropriately, they played 'Blue Bonnets Over the Border'. This was followed later by a freight train arriving in the American sector with 769 tons of coal. For the so-called third arm of supply – the airlift – it was just another day of unbroken operations.

The 323-day Soviet blockade of Berlin was over.

No one would question that, for the Western occupation powers, the lifting of the blockade was a diplomatic victory. The Allies were adamant that they would not sit around a table with the Soviets until they removed the blockade; they would not negotiate under the duress of the Berlin crisis.

But there was also a popular school of thought that viewed Russian actions in Berlin as intimidation bordering on blatant aggression. Moscow never conceded that the blockade was illegal and inhumane. The Allies would also not be deceived by Russian proposals for the withdrawal of occupation troops, as this would leave Germany at the mercy of substantial numbers of Soviet armed and trained paramilitary police. The forthcoming foreign ministers' meeting would require a united front and common purpose should the West wish to retain the initiative.

And in the interim, Soviet zonal border authorities reverted to political gamesmanship to show they still controlled the flow of traffic. In seemingly deliberate acts of bureaucratic demands, road and rail transport backed up for considerable distances awaiting import/export

Above left: No time was wasted for the British to have their scientists work on Hitler's V-2 rockets.

Above right: Water in many parts of Berlin was unsuitable for drinking.

formalities and clearance. The Soviet transport chief, Major General Kvashnin, when told of the border backlog, was reported to have simply shrugged his shoulders, saying, 'This is a matter for the economic department.'

In an ongoing game of subterfuge, Moscow would not stand down, especially with the added military and political embarrassment that such a move would bring. The unforgiving, unyielding Stalin would never contemplate relinquishing the spoils of war over which he firmly believed he had sole ownership. He had lifted the blockade, but his was not a magnanimous or philanthropic act. History would attest to this.

By October 1949, Hitler's Germany was firmly divided between East and West: ideologically, militarily and physically. In the first quarter of 1952, acting on Foreign Minister Vyshinsky's initiative, the East Germans erected a barbed-wire fence along the border separating the two German states. Four years later, there followed a major tightening up of people movement between the two sectors in Berlin, particularly to stem the flow from East to West.

On 13 August, Moscow reasserted its dominance of the Eastern bloc to ensure total doctrinal compliance of those to the east of the Iron Curtain. A heavily armed barrier definitively split Berlin. This was in readiness for the erection of the notorious 140-kilometre-long Berlin Wall.

On 26 June 1963, American President John F. Kennedy famously told a 450,000-strong crowd in Berlin that '*Ich bin ein Berliner*' – 'I am a citizen of Berlin'. The ill-fated president, in a subtle challenge to the Kremlin, proclaimed that, 'All free men, wherever they may live, are citizens of Berlin.'

US President Ronald Reagan stood at the iconic Brandenburg Gate twenty-four years later challenging, 'General Secretary [Mikhail] Gorbachev, if you seek peace, if you seek prosperity for the Soviet Union and Eastern Europe, if you seek liberalisation, come here to this gate. Mr Gorbachev, open this gate. Mr Gorbachev, tear down this Wall.'

The Wall came down on 9 November 1989, reuniting a city that had remained forcibly divided for forty years. The Soviet stranglehold on Berlin finally ended.

AIRLIFT GOES INTO COLD STORAGE

Final plans to suspend the airlift were announced here today.

Simultaneously, a huge 'airlift parade' was held at Passenberg, in the British zone, in memory of the sixty-seven men – British, American and German – who have lost their lives flying supplies to Berlin.

The suspension, which comes into effect on Monday, is made possible by the large stocks which have now been accumulated. Supplies for five months are available, and in the event of a new blockade, there will be a skeleton air force and enough air bases kept in order for the lift to begin again. If all goes well, rail, barge and road facilities will meet Berlin's needs.

The lift has brought 2,214,075 short tons of goods into Berlin in 274,718 flights.

Of the sixty-seven killed, twenty-nine were British. At Passenberg, hundreds of servicemen of the three Western Occupying Powers marched past, and the salute was taken by the Air Officer Commanding-in-Chief, Air Marshal Williams.

Aberdeen Journal, Saturday, 30 July 1949

7. AT WHAT COST?

'Watching it work one was always conscious that it was a high price to pay to beat the blockade, in British and American lives as well as money'.

Captain Michael Bowen, 44th Royal Tank Regiment

In Luftwaffe-traumatised Britain, where the rationing of fuel and certain basic foodstuffs remained a way of daily life for most, sympathy, let alone empathy, for the distant capital of the much-loathed Adolf Hitler, was in limited supply. In a letter to the editor of the *Western Morning News* of 28 September 1948, reader Jas. F. Jackson of Goodrington Sands, near Paignton in Devon, castigated the government's questionable involvement in Berlin:

Sir: The monetary cost of the Berlin air lift matters little, because whatever might have been saved would only have been wasted on some silly Socialist schemes. What does matter very much is the total loss of 9,000 tons of fuel, to date, and the steady wearing out of hundreds of aero-engines, not to mention the continuing strain on aircrews, while Stalin goes on building up his resources. And, presumably, the process is to continue indefinitely, while the Western Powers' case wanders through the circumlocutory departments of that international lost property office commonly known as the UNO.

The shell of Berlin's Anhalter Station.

Worst of all, after shouting 'No discussions under duress,' the Powers have gone on doing it for seven weeks, scurrying backwards and forwards from the Kremlin, as if they had forgotten how they were fooled in 1939, while Stalin was polishing up the Order of Lenin for the manly chest of Comrade Ribbentrop [Nazi Reich Minister for Foreign Affairs, SS-Obergruppenführer Joachim von Ribbentrop]. How very pleased with himself Stalin must feel to find again that there appears to be no discoverable limit to the credulity of the West.

Statistically, almost 278,000 sorties were flown during the blockade, by aircrews from the United States Air Force, the British Royal Air Force, the Royal Canadian Air Force, the Royal Australian Air Force, the Royal New Zealand Air Force, and the South African Air Force, ferrying some 2.3 million tons into the beleaguered Berlin. Of this tonnage, 1.5 million tons alone was coal. A staggering 124.4 million miles were flown. There were 17 American and eight British aircraft accidents, resulting in a death toll of 83: 39 British, 31 American and 13 German civilians. There were more than 730 recorded incidents of Soviet harassment that took place as relief aircraft flew over the Soviet zone.

In financial terms, the British parliament was informed in June 1949 that the airlift had cost the British taxpayer £8,600,000, which equated to almost 24 percent of total freight carried by the Allies. The final cost to the British taxpayer was, however, £17 million. The United States injected US$350 million into the operation, with an added cost to Western Germany of DM115 million. In today's inflation-adjusted terms, the total cost of the airlift amounts to more than US$2 billion.

Sherman tanks navigate their way through Nuremburg's old inner city, reduced to rubble by Allied bombing.

A severely damaged church in Berlin.

On 10 July 1951, to the strains of a German soldier's song, 'I Had a Comrade', played by the Berlin Police Band, the city's mayor, Dr Ernst Reuter, unveiled the Airlift Memorial at Tempelhof Airfield.

The 63-feet-high, three-pronged white concrete edifice sits on a black basalt base. The memorial – *Luftbrückendenkmal* – was, because of its shape, dubbed the 'hunger rake', *Hungerharke*, by the capital's burghers. An identical memorial was also erected at the Rhein Main Air Base, Frankfurt.

Bearing the inscription, 'In memory of all those who lost their lives for the freedom of Berlin during the blockade', the memorial base carries the names of 39 British and 31 American airmen, and five Germans who lost their lives during the operations.

Roll of Honour
American

First Lieutenant Ralph H. Boyd	12 January 1949
Aviation Machinist Mate Third Class Harry R. Crites, Jnr	11 December 1948
Captain Joel M. DeVolentine	24 August 1948
Major Edwin C. Diltz	24 August 1948
First Lieutenant Eugene S. Erickson	18 October 1948
Mr Karl V. Hagen	8 July 1948
First Lieutenant Willis F. Hargis	5 December 1948
Temporary Sergeant Herbert F. Heinig	12 July 1949
Captain William R. Howard	24 August 1948
First Lieutenant Charles H. King	24 July 1948

First Lieutenant Craig B. Ladd	12 January 1949
Second Lieutenant Donald J. Leemon	12 July 1949
First Lieutenant William T. Lucas	24 August 1948
First Lieutenant Robert C. von Luehrte	12 July 1949
Private First Class Johnny T. Orms	2 October 1948
Captain Billy E. Phelps	5 December 1948
Technical Sergeant Charles L. Putnam	12 January 1949
Captain William A. Rathgeber	7 January 1949
First Lieutenant George B. Smith	8 July 1948
First Lieutenant Royce C. Stephens	4 March 1949
Private First Class Ronald E. Stone	7 January 1949
First Lieutenant Robert W. Stuber	25 July 1948
Corporal Norbert H. Theis	7 January 1948
Captain James A. Vaughan	18 October 1948
Sergeant Bernard J. Watkins	7 January 1949
First Lieutenant Robert P. Weaver	18 January 1949
Technical Sergeant Lloyd G. Wells	5 December 1948
First Lieutenant Lowell A. Wheaton, Jnr	7 January 1949
First Lieutenant Leland V. Williams	8 July 1948
Sergeant Richard Winter	18 October 1948
First Lieutenant Richard M. Wurgel	7 January 1949

British and Commonwealth

Engineer Officer John Anderson	30 April 1949
Navigation Officer Alan J. Burton	22 November 1948
Navigation Officer Edward E. Carroll	30 April 1949
Navigation Officer Michael E. Casey	22 November 1948
Captain William Cusak	22 November 1948
Flying Officer Ian R. Donaldson	16 July 1949
Sergeant Frank Dowling	17 November 1948
Signalman Class Two Alexander Dunsire	16 July 1949
Radio Officer Peter J. Edwards	15 March 1949
Captain Robert J. Freight	21 March 1949
Engineer Class Two Roy R. Gibbs	16 July 1949
Navigator Class Two Lawrence E.H. Gilbert	19 September 1948
Captain Cecil Golding	15 March 1949
Ground Engineer Patrick J. Griffin	15 January 1949
Signalman Class One John E. Grout	24 January 1949
Captain Reginald M.W. Heath DFC	22 November 1948
Flight Lieutenant Geoffrey Kell	19 September 1948
Captain William R.D. Lewis	30 April 1949
Signalman Class Three Philip A. Louch	17 November 1948
First Officer Henry T. Newman	15 March 1949
Ground Engineer Edward O'Neil	15 January 1949
Navigator Class One William G. Page	16 July 1949

Engineer Officer Henry Patterson	21 March 1949
Master Signaller Alan Penny AFC	22 March 1949
Flight Lieutenant Mel J. Quinn, Royal Australian Air Force	22 March 1949
Flying Officer Kenneth A. Reeves	22 March 1949
Radio Officer Dornford W. Robertson	22 November 1948
Flight Engineer Kenneth A. Seaborne DFM	22 November 1948
Navigation Officer Patrick L. Sharp DFC	21 March 1949
Ground Engineer Theodor Supernatt	15 January 1949
Captain Cyril Taylor DFC, AFM	22 November 1949
Flight Lieutenant Hugh W. Thomson MC, DFC	19 September 1948
Sergeant Joseph Toal	16 July 1948
Signalman Class Two Sidney M.L. Towersey	19 September 1948
Pilot Class One Francis I. Trevona	17 November 1948
Captain Clement W. Uttig	8 December 1948
Engineer Class Two Ernest W. Watson	19 September 1948
Flight Lieutenant John G. Wilkins	17 November 1948
Radio Officer Kenneth G. Wood	30 April 1949

Berlin Air Disaster

On 5 April 1948, a British European Airways Vickers VC 1B Viking (G-AIVP), en route from Hamburg to Berlin, collided in the air with a Soviet Yak-3 fighter, killing the crew of four and all ten passengers. The Viking had been on a routine flight from Northolt to Gatow, Berlin, when a Russian fighter from Dahlhof in the Soviet zone flew across the Viking's nose, causing both aircraft to crash in flames.

The crew were all former members of the Royal Air Force:
Captain John Ralph from Middlesex
First Officer Norman B. Merrington from Buckinghamshire
Radio Officer Charles Manser from London
Steward Leonard G. Goodman from London
Passengers:
Mr Valdemar Hald from Australia
Sergeant Pintus from the USA
Mrs J. Clough from London
Miss J. Shea from London (daughter of General Sir John S.M. Shea GCB, KCMG, DSO)
Mr J.E. Roberts (Postal and Telecommunications Branch, Control Commission)
Mr S.J. Stocking from Surrey
Captain I.G.A. Flemings from Dunbartonshire
Mr Robert Collier from Kent (British United Press)
Mr H. Read-Hahm from Middlesex
Mr Edward G. Lewin from Middlesex

Few would argue, however, that the greatest cost was that borne by the more than two million residents who called Berlin home. Already left demoralised, hungry and homeless by the horrors of sustained Allied bombing of their city – 65,000 tons of bombs in two years – in a

The Berlin Airlift
Memorial at the
National Memorial
Arboretum.

space of two weeks, Soviet forces threw 40,000 tons of explosive ordnance at the benumbed citizens. As the city fell to the Red Army, degradation swamped the Germans: mass rape, humiliation and slaughter at the hands of the Vodka-fuelled enemy knew no bounds. *Selbstmord* – suicide – was not uncommon: an estimated 4,000 civilians took their own lives and those of their families to avoid the advancing Russians.

Even with the cessation of hostilities in May 1945, the death toll as a result of disease continued to rise. From 1940 to 1944, Berlin's death rate had risen to 15 per 1,000, but in the second half of 1945, this had spiralled to 53 per 1,000. In July alone, the newborn mortality rate was 66 percent.

The new communist masters left those Germans that fate had trapped in the Soviet sector in no doubt that they were now the subjugated. Lifestyle, behaviour and culture would be at the sole discretion of the Socialist government. The Soviet authorities would not defile their persons by burying German dead – the citizens had to bury their own. As a consequence, the corpses of German soldiers and civilians were generally buried in shallow graves randomly dug in a patch of soil nearest the body. Many were not interred, and by 1949, the scattered, sun-bleached bones of German war dead remained a common site in East Berlin.

Herr Willy Brandt, Chancellor of the Federal Republic of Germany from 1969 to 1974, was an assistant to the mayor of Western Berlin during the period of the blockade. During the war, the future recipient of the Nobel Peace Prize fled Nazi Germany to Norway and Sweden, where he adopted the pseudonym Willy Brandt instead of his real name: Herbert Ernst Karl Frahm.

Returning to Berlin after the war, Brandt would later give an insight into German life during the Soviet blockade:

At the beginning of the blockade, the supplies in the west sectors were enough to guarantee the barely sufficient rations for approximately four weeks at maximum. In the first months, just enough food was brought in by air to secure the further issue of the rations and to save the Berliners from starving to death – but hunger they could not be spared.

The stock of coal was supposed to last for thirty days, but it was impossible to replenish it to the same extent as the urgently needed food. Apartments and the greater part of offices – even the administration buildings – could no longer be heated. Every family got for the whole winter an allotment of twenty-five pounds of coal and three boxes of wood. Some fuel was smuggled in by black marketeers. Most of the families were glad when they could keep one room of their apartment moderately warm for a few hours of the day. Fortunately, the winter was not particularly severe.

Electric current was only available for four hours daily, usually in two periods of two hours each. These periods came at different times of day in different sections of the city, and people had to rise at odd hours in order to take advantage of the available current.

The Berliners did not waver, though in addition to hunger and cold – particularly in the first months of the blockade – they were subjected to a vicious fear propaganda. The Soviets declared that all of Berlin was theirs, and their newspapers in German language didn't cease to foretell the realization of that claim. They spread rumours of different kinds, they didn't spare threats and intimidations. Thus, here and there, doubts arose as to whether one would be able to resist the Russian pressure in the long run. The retaliation and vengeance in case of a defeat would be terrible.

(J.M. Hanhimäki & O.A. Westad (eds.), *The Cold War: a history in documents and eyewitness accounts* (Oxford: 2004))

ACKNOWLEDGEMENTS

My personal sincere thanks, as always, to the unfailing support from friend, fellow historian and former brother-in-arms, Colonel Dudley Wall. Not only is his military knowledge of significant value, but his drawings and images of militaria from his private collection contribute a rich and unique element to this publication.

Thank you Chris and Kerrin Cocks for your production work on this book, and especially for believing in me.

Thank you Philip Nixon for the splendid photograph of the Berlin Airlift Memorial, at the National Memorial Arboretum, Alrewas, which has been used as the frontispiece and on the back cover.

I extend my gratitude to the British and American branches of the Berlin Airlift Association for their magnanimous and generous contributions.

Source material has been drawn from The British Newspaper Archive and the contemporary Second World War periodicals, *The War* and *The Illustrated War*.

ABOUT THE AUTHOR

Born and raised in Southern Rhodesia, historian, researcher, copy-editor and author, Gerry van Tonder came to Britain in 1999, settling in Derby, the city of his wife Tracey's birth. In Rhodesia, he completed 18 months' national service during the guerrilla war of the 1970s, before reading for a BA (Honours) degree at the University of Rhodesia. He served as a Liaison & Returning Officer during the Zimbabwean election of 1980.

Gerry has co-authored *Rhodesian Combined Forces Roll of Honour 1966–1981*, the landmark *Rhodesia Regiment 1899–1981* – a copy of this book was presented to the regiment's former colonel-in-chief, Her Majesty the Queen – and *North of the Red Line: Recollections of the Border War by Members of the SADF and SWATF 1966–1989*. He is author of *Rhodesian Native Regiment/Rhodesian African Rifles Book of Remembrance* and is working on a further Rhodesian title, *Operation Lighthouse*, an account of a paramilitary government ministry in the 1970s' insurgency. He has written three local history books: *Derby in 50 Buildings*, *Chesterfield's Military Heritage* and *Mansfield through Time*. For Pen & Sword he has written two Cold War titles, *Berlin Blockade: Soviet Chokehold and the Great Allied Airlift 1948–1949* and *Malayan Emergency: Triumph of the Running Dogs 1948–1960*, as well as *Nottingham's Military Legacy* and *Echoes of the Coventry Blitz*. Gerry has his own website www.rhodesiansoldier.com.